THE DESIGN ENTREPRENEUR

TURNING GRAPHIC DESIGN INTO GOODS THAT SELL

ROCKPORT PUBLISHERS

D0580647

First published in the United States of America by

Rockport Publishers, a member of

Quayside Publishing Group

100 Cummings Center

Suite 406-L

Beverly, Massachusetts 01915-6101

Telephone: (978) 282-9590

Fax: (978) 283-2742

www.rockpub.com

Library of Congress Cataloging-in-Publication Data

Heller, Steven.

The design entrepreneur : turning graphic design into goods that sell /
by Steven Heller and Lita Talarico.

p. cm.

Includes index.

ISBN 1-59253-421-X

1. Commercial art—Marketing. 2. Graphic arts—Marketing. 3. Entrepreneurship—Handbooks, manuals, etc. 4. New business enterprises—Handbooks, manuals, etc.
I. Talarico, Lita. II. Title.

NC1001.H44 2008

741.6068'8—dc22   2007052144

ISBN-13: 978-1-59253-421-0

ISBN-10: 1-59253-421-X

10 9 8 7 6 5 4 3 2 1

Design: Rick Landers

Printed in China

CONTENTS

232.
ONLINE
RESOURCES

INTRODUCTION

THE "I CAN DO IT ALL" GENERATION

It is not a new idea, though it is a revolutionary one. Modern design entrepreneurship has been around at least since the late nineteenth century when William Morris' Arts and Crafts workshops, manned by ardent artisans and designers, hand produced everything from typefaces to books to furniture destined for sale in a marketplace of special devotees. The movement migrated to Aurora, New York, where the Morris disciples, Elbert Hubbard and his Roycrofters adherents sold a wide range of products through catalogs and stores. The tradition evolved with the Weiner Werkstätte, Deutsche Werbund, and Bauhaus, to name a few progressive design movements and schools, where *gesamtkunstwerk* (the total work of art) was the mantra for those adept at creating a variety of forms with different media for mainstream markets.

"...designers have traditionally been brought in at the end, rather than the beginning, of a product (certainly after the fundamental decisions are made) and hired to package, rather than conceive."

Even the nascent Soviet Union had its revolutionary Productivists who produced designed objects for sale to the masses, albeit for the benefit of the Bolshevik transformation. In line with the mandates of capitalism in the United States, Contempora, a design collective that included the contributions of poster and type designer Lucian Bernhard, graphic artist Rockwell Kent, and furniture designer Paul T. Frankl, among others, produced unique textiles, home accessories, and *objets d'art* sold in stores and galleries. During the early twentieth century, various other graphic, product, furniture, and fashion designers commingled their talents and crossed their disciplines to produce wares unbound by client interference but receptive to free market needs. Although the term we use now was not necessarily applied, these *design entrepreneurs*—what might well be defined as risk-taking, business-minded visionaries—dreamt up concepts that largely fulfilled their own creative and profit-driven needs.

DRIVE MAKES ALL THE DIFFERENCE

Whether personal or collective, *drive* is the common denominator of all entrepreneurial pursuit; of course, then comes the brilliant idea; and finally, the fervent wherewithal to make and market the result. It is a simple equation: d (drive) + b (brilliant) = c (critical mass). In terms of physics, two forces—will and intelligence—must be fused in order to generate enough energy to take the entrepreneurial plunge and it's not always easy. Many designers have good, even great ideas, but odds are most of these will simply remain notions rather than become concrete products. One reason is the apparent in-ability to move from notion to concept or from concept to product because designers have a perceived lack of expertise. That is nothing to be ashamed of given that they are good at solving problems that involve making aesthetic decisions, but invariably rely on others to do the "heavy lifting" of manufacturing and investing. Moreover, designers have traditionally been brought in at the end, rather than the beginning, of a product (certainly after the fundamental decisions are made) and hired to package, rather than conceive.

As the design disciplines become more interrelated, a rising tide of "I can do it all," or a sense of overarching confidence, has washed over the new generation of designers—at least judging from the in-creased number of design entrepreneurs. They are no longer reticent about jumping— sometimes head first —into other (albeit usually related) fields if their business idea demands it. Design students, for example,

Two forces—will and intelligence—must be fused in order to generate enough energy to take the entrepreneurial plunge and it's not always easy.

are not only prepared to make a well-rounded portfolio showing evidence of requisite skill sets, they are encouraged to produce ideas that have entrepreneurial resonance. Why should invention be limited to the old when, in fact, the young may have a clearer idea of what is necessary to fulfill their generation's needs. So design students—not only in the product area, but all realms—are told to make the widget that will turn the world on its ear.

THE VIABLE IDEA

How does one know whether an entrepreneurial idea is viable? Obviously, not every concept is as good as one thinks it is (and some are even better). But not every idea has to be a cure for the common cold either. Some successful business concepts are viable novelties—games, for example—while others are more lasting, like a furniture or fashion line. Some notions are meant to be independently sold in the market without the benefit of a middleman or investor; others are in need of greater support and financial backing. There are many ways to be a design entrepreneur and many different kinds of products that fall under the rubric.

In 1998, we launched the MFA Designer as Author program at the School of Visual Arts in New York (which is alternatively referred to as the Designer as Entrepreneur)—the first design entrepreneur program on a Masters Degree level. The *big idea* behind this is relatively straightforward: Designers have skills and talents that enable them to conceive products, identify the audience, and engage in the prototyping and fabrication. While this concept is simple, the act of fulfillment is more difficult. Actually

developing even the good idea—which is not to say all good ideas start out that way—is a fairly difficult evolutionary process during which time the entrepreneur must determine in what form to best launch a product (and promote it, too). The happy surprise is that a vast majority of our MFA students have the chops to succeed (see some projects in Chapter 1, page 15). And this supported our belief that the entrepreneurial pursuit, something of a cousin to the highly popular D.I.Y. (do-it-yourself) practice of late, is on the upswing.

BECOMING A DESIGN ENTREPRENEUR

This book is a fervent testament to the proposition that a greater number of designers—decidedly aided by computers and other accessible technologies and materials—are more actively seeking full- and part-time roles as entrepreneurs than ever before. To underscore this claim, we've assembled two groups within which are various subsets.

The first group is our own MFA graduates, including many who have progressed further with their entrepreneurial thesis projects. Some are in the marketplace now, while others are in the pipeline. Our greatest accomplishment, Deborah Adler's prescription drug labeling and packaging system for Target stores, began as a thesis topic and evolved into a full-fledged rollout in 2005 and 2006. What made this entrepreneurial was that it was self-generated, rather than a commission from Target. Adler saw a need and decided to fill it. Only after an alternative was found did she look for its corporate home.

The second group consists of design

"A design entrepreneur has to be committed to creating and finding a niche for a product that has some value and is able to see it reach that audience."

entrepreneurs—either designers who have gone out on their own in search of a market, or non-designer producers who have nonetheless rooted their entrepreneurship on the necessity of design and designer partners. The vast majority are designers of all disciplines and illustrators, some of whom have immersed themselves in designing their products as the answer to their entrepreneurial need and a few others whose byproducts will thrive as market-satisfying products.

The term *design entrepreneur* runs the risk of becoming a new buzzword, a catchall for anyone who develops and sells any designed trinket. In fact, there are rigors involved. A design entrepreneur has to be committed to creating (and sometimes failing) and finding a niche for a product that has some value (at least for the audience) and is able to see it reach that audience. Just making some fun doodad and putting it on a shelf is not enough. The design entrepreneur must take the leap away from the safety of the traditional designer role into the precarious territory where the public decides what works and what does not.

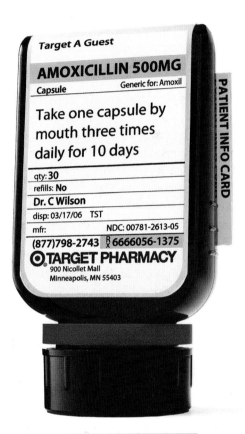

The distinctive Target prescription bottle and labeling system designed by Deborah Adler began as an entrepreneurial thesis and was turned into a real product when her unique, "big" idea was wed to a corporate decision to make a radical change.

CHAPTER 1

CONCEIVING
IDEAS

During the mid-1950s, an era-defining phenomenon overtook the advertising and design fields; it was called the "Big Idea" revolution. Although no shots were fired or governments overthrown—and maybe the word revolution is more hyperbole than truth—nonetheless, the revolutionary spirit was consistent with the innovative philosophy underscoring the Big Idea. It was certainly a coming-of-age period of American consumerism and prosperity, when advertising and design were more than the process of making things look good. The result had to sound, read, and look *smart*. Indeed, smart ideas were supreme, and everything else was merely fluff.

In advertising, this meant clever copy wed to eye-catching (and mind-stimulating) images; in graphic design, it meant an increase in, among other perceptual stimulants, visual puns (which unlike verbal puns were actually sophisticated, often layered graphic concepts). The "Big Idea" movement built up momentum until sometime in the late 1980s, when it ran out of steam. The consuming public became used to the idea of big ideas, and the ideas themselves were not as big as they once were anyway.

This is when designers instinctively knew that they were ready for an infusion of a new kind of creative energy. It was, therefore, about the time when the new Big Idea of conceiving entrepreneurial ideas started percolating. While only a few intrepid souls initially went out on proverbial limbs to invent, produce, and distribute their own products, the way was paved for others to move forward. Today, the entrepreneurial spirit is the *new* Big Idea. This book examines how well (and intrepidly) designers have mastered the new creative force and as such is a guide to becoming an expert at conceiving ideas.

IS EVERYONE AN ENTREPRENEUR?

Not everyone has the gift to conceive or detect the Big Idea, but all designers have the potential to develop entrepreneurships simply by virtue of their ability to generate big and small ideas and then—and this is the truly big part—fulfill the promise by making them real. While in the past designers were hired to make other peoples' ideas concrete, in this new entrepreneurial environment, designers (and design students) are thinking, conceiving, and making their own products. Of course, this does not preclude the traditional role of designers as serving clients, but it does suggest that the alternative—once the exception to the rule—is becoming more commonplace. The designer as entrepreneur actually has an advantage over the non-design entrepreneur who must employ others to manufacture, package, brand, and promote. Even if the designer subcontracts these tasks to others, he does so from a position of complete understanding of the media and materials involved.

Yet before even considering the back end, the front end, or the conception of ideas, there is the entry point. And the question most asked of creative people, as well as those who choose to self-generate marketable products, is where do said ideas come from, and how? While there is no magic pill—everyone draws upon different stimuli for ideas—there are some useful procedures to follow when starting out as a design entrepreneur.

CLEARING THE DECKS TO MAKE SPACE IN THE MIND

The very first thing to do is so simple it needs no explanation (but then again it can't hurt to say it): *Make sure the mind is clear of client-driven problems and solutions so it can be free to create original ideas.* If one does not think conventionally, the result may be surprising. While surprise is a double-edged sword (being too far ahead of the curve has its drawbacks), it is also what triggers inspiration both in creator and consumer. In any case, surprising or not, the entrepreneurial idea usually comes, at least at the outset, from a personal (or autobiographical) perspective. For instance, when Deborah Adler was a student in the MFA Design program at the School of Visual Arts (devoted to training design entrepreneurs), her thesis, to create a safe means of labeling and packaging prescription drugs, came directly from a life-threatening experience that occurred when her grandmother took the wrong medication. Although she had long believed that common drug containers were dangerously ambiguous, personal contact with the problem triggered action. Adler's response is one of many student and professional responses to real-life events resulting in the need to fix things.

There are, of course, other personal reasons to invent or reinvent. The driving urge may stem from something that has been tucked away in the subconscious and may explode in some instant burst of inspiration. Or it may be something that has been gestating for a long time, waiting for the right moment and place to emerge. There are also degrees and levels of big ideas. Some might want to invent the better mousetrap, while others are happy to create something less grandiose but decidedly useful.

Inventors tend to invent because they have the uncontrollable urge to make something that will change life in some way. Whatever the primary reasons, the human mind is always coming up with ideas, and the first important step in entrepreneurial creation is to take some of those ad hoc thoughts to the next level.

So the second step for the design entrepreneur is editing. It is important to determine on which ideas it really is worth investing personal time, and which ideas should be foisted on a world that already has tapped many of its resources to the limit. Not every idea is good, even if it seems to be brilliant at first blush, and it is important to be circumspect. Just because they are self-generated ideas does not mean they are the best solutions for a particular problem. Editing means being wary enough to do

what designers do as a matter of course when parsing ideas for a client: selecting two or three ideas and then asking hard questions about viability, feasibility, and acceptability. Can the idea really have legs as an entity? Is the idea something that an audience will want to purchase? Is it possible to efficiently and effectively fabricate and produce the idea for a market? Will the idea add something of value to others? Before wasting time, effort, and materials, the design entrepreneur must make evaluative decisions based on fact and anecdote. If the answers to these fundamental questions are affirmative, it may still be a gamble, but a reasonable one.

The next step then is to test the theory of the idea by making effective indicators—a prototype or some other physical mechanism that allows the creator and the consumer a chance to make more definitive determinations. While this may sound clinically formulaic, the fact is that the big idea is only as good as the product itself. For example, the crazily drawn conceptual machinery seen in the work of Rube Goldberg, the legendary 1930s American cartoonist, was fun to see in drawings but would have been impossible to mass-produce as viable products. His cartoons satirized the stereotype of an eccentric inventor who made otherwise simple ideas into complex mélanges of gears and conveyers, serving as something of a cautionary lesson for those who want to produce viable products.

While big ideas may certainly be complex, the most effective are those that, in product form, are reduced to comparative simplicity. Conversely, Leonardo da Vinci also drew speculative inventions, like flying machines, that seemed inconceivable at the time, yet history showed they were quite prescient. This, too, is a cautionary lesson—to stick with existing technologies even if the idea is visionary. The trick to being a design entrepreneur is having a keen awareness of what ideas are truly possible to bring to fruition.

KNOWING WHEN AN IDEA IS THE BEST IDEA

Sometimes only a best friend (or worst enemy) will provide the most honest evaluation of a big idea. Casual friends (or those who want to curry favor) or family (who are blindly supportive or habitually critical) will rarely say, "That idea stinks," or, "Good thing you kept your day job," or variants thereof. That is why it is important to seek some respected, if not expert, critical reaction to an idea before investing in it any further. Taking into account that objective critics are not always correct (or visionary), the odds are that their responses will have some bearing on the success or failure of a project.

At the School of Visual Arts' MFA Design Program, each thesis must be vetted by committees of faculty and expert advisors prior to their agreeing that an idea should move to the next stage of fabrication. In addition, surveys (see Chapter 2) are required to determine if the average consumer would be at all interested in the idea. Whether one is a graduate student or not, deciding on which idea is the best idea demands some testing. In fact, far from putting the damper on a good idea, tests may help finesse or perfect an idea.

Sometimes a big idea doesn't need to be transformed beyond minor tweaking.

Being focused on an outcome may bolster a good idea (and a good idea can fail if that focus does not exist); this cannot be overstated or repeated too often.

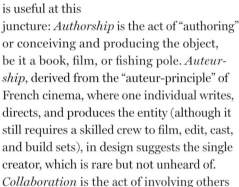

AUTHORSHIP AND COLLABORATION

Defining terms is useful at this juncture: *Authorship* is the act of "authoring" or conceiving and producing the object, be it a book, film, or fishing pole. *Auteurship*, derived from the "auteur-principle" of French cinema, where one individual writes, directs, and produces the entity (although it still requires a skilled crew to film, edit, cast, and build sets), in design suggests the single creator, which is rare but not unheard of. *Collaboration* is the act of involving others with the final outcome to engage in the entire process.

Being a design author/entrepreneur does not mean one must be a lone creator toiling away in the proverbial artist's garret. With so many resources and so much media available today, collaboration is not just a luxury but a necessity. Most big ideas demand a concerted involvement of vendors, fabricators, strategists, promoters, and more. The false notion that one can be a super designer/entrepreneur and do it all is fool hardy, if not impossible. While sole ownership of an idea (and of the patent or registration) is possible, embracing the best team is more important than any initial ego gratification. Remember, most design is a collaborative activity. Few designers can develop products on their own. But if all the skills are in place, the majority of the authorship can be attributed to the conceiver.

The rule of thumb for designer entrepreneurs is this: Rely on those who will make the products into realities. A big idea, as well as a small, good idea, is not very big or very good if it sits lifelessly on paper. Collaboration is not a sin.

PERSONAL EXPRESSION

When looking through stores of any kind, one sees a remarkable array of products that appeal to the consumer on various levels of interest and experience. Some clearly fill a practical need, while others trigger emotional, indeed passionate responses. Just as the products touch an expressive chord in the consumer, they emerged from an expressive place in the designer. A design entrepreneur should be cautiously circumspect in determining whether their personal passions are viably marketable products, but neither should one ever discard pure expression as being too self-indulgent. As stated above, many of the best entrepreneurial wares derive from an autobiographical place. Sometimes they seem extremely personal, but other times they can also be universalized.

For some products to succeed, the quirky must somehow be second to functionality, but for others, the individual hand and mind is what creates the appeal. A balance between the two is always necessary. But if one is to be an author/entrepreneur, it is useful to allow that personal expression to come through, at least at the beginning of the process. Then see how the market responds and finesse accordingly.

{ TAREK ATRISSI

ORIGINAL, CONTEMPORARY ARABIC TYPEFACES

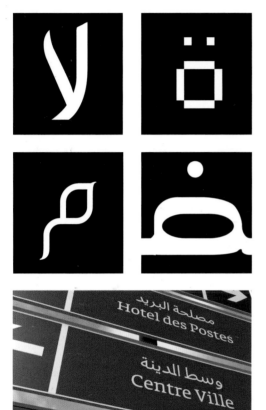

(Top) Selection of Arabic typefaces and typefaces (bottom) as they appear on city signage. Design: Tarek Atrissi

PURPOSE: The Arabic fonts we develop at Tarek Atrissi Design are meant to provide the new generation of graphic designers in the Arab world, and all users of the Arabic script, with a set of modern Arabic fonts that have a contemporary feel and provide more typographic possibilities in daily design practice. While the fonts are inspired by the tradition and roots of Arabic calligraphy, they are not limited by it. Through different concepts and inspirations, the fonts provide users a fresh look and feel and aim to leave a mark in the Arabic typographic landscape.

BACK STORY: Developing Arabic typefaces started at the very roots of a problem: As a graphic designer mainly involved in projects with an Arabic flavor, I have always faced considerable difficulties finding the right fonts for projects I was working on. On the one hand, the availability was very limited, and the font palette was not as wide as is the case with Latin fonts. On the other hand, most of the fonts were very traditional, often imitating the historical and rich Arabic calligraphy, but failing to preserve its fluidity and beauty, in addition to often not being suitable for contemporary design projects. So with every new project that I worked on in my studio, I often developed custom lettering for specific titles, headers, mastheads, and typographic titles. The custom lettering habit led to developing typefaces for us to use in certain projects. Eventually, with much demand and a lot of interest, I started making these fonts available for other designers to license.

DESIGN: Because we are developing several fonts, my approach changes and constantly evolves, particularly when I see the font taking on a life of its own when used in the real world.

{ PETER BUCHANAN-SMITH
SPECK

(Left) Cover and (right) spread from *Speck*. Published by Princeton Architectural Press. Design: Peter Buchanan-Smith; photography: Stacy Greene.

PURPOSE: *Speck* is meant to inspire people to look more closely at what they normally see and to find meaning in these things. *Speck* was not only meant to be a beautiful object to adorn one's coffee table, but more ambitiously, I hoped it would be the start of a community of like-minded people, the start of a "movement" of sorts.

BACK STORY: *Speck* was originally the product of my fascination with the notion of "the everyday"; something that caught my fancy while I was a student at the MFA Designer as Author program at SVA. Elements of this theme could be found in the work of many of the artists that inspired me at the time: Marcel Duchamp, Fluxus, the Situationists, Andy Warhol, Joseph Cornell, and Claes Oldenburg, among others. During and after the making of a 60-page prototype (my master's thesis), I noticed that unexpected people (mainly friends who were not designers, artists, or creative types) responded favorably to the stories I was telling. These endorsements, along with favorable reviews by my colleagues and instructors at SVA, reinforced my belief that *Speck* could not only be a real book someday, but more importantly, it could have a following.

OUTCOME: *Speck* was published in the spring of 2001. It was remaindered in 2007. As a designer with various projects under my belt, *Speck* remains my most valued portfolio piece, sometimes simply because it is one of the few projects that has my name on the front. But most gratifying is that it actually made some lasting impression on people and maybe the publishing/design landscape at large. People still write to me to ask about it, strangers tell me they bought it (and read it!), and I often hear that students use it as a creative resource.

{ LUISA GLORIA MOTA VELASCO

SAN HONESTO

PURPOSE: San Honesto's purpose is to create awareness of corruption and to stop it by believing in ourselves, by creating a positive change within us, and believing that it can be eradicated if we stop blaming others and start accepting that each of us are part of the problem.

BACK STORY: I was born in Mexico City and have been living with corruption, injustice, discrimination, and lying my entire life. But I have also lived surrounded by magic, miracles, and faith. I have seen people cured by faith rather than with medicine. This is where I came up with the idea of using faith to stop corruption. I have seen miracles happen, and I would love to witness the miracle of stopping corruption! There is a saint for almost everything: the saint that brings love, the saint of drug dealers and prostitutes, the saint of death, the saint of animals, and the saint of lost things. The only saint that we are missing is the saint against corruption: San Honesto.

DESIGN: San Honesto's visual image comes from different parts of the legend: He is wearing eighteenth century dress typical for a Mexican olive picker—a white tunic with a hay sombrero, black belt, and a serape with a mandala pattern on his shoulder. He used to work in a maguey and olive hacienda; the olive branch can be seen on his hat. The maguey cactus with fearful spines symbolizes corruption; San Honesto is standing on it, fearless of getting hurt. Two elements represent the collision of Spanish (olives) and Aztec (maguey) cultures, creating the new Mexican culture. He is holding a bowl of water symbolizing transparency. His face, which is a mirror, represents facing yourself, starting the change within yourself instead of blaming others. The last step was to create related nonreligious and religious products that felt familiar to people and that are used for other saints and deities.

(Top) San Honesto Logo and (bottom) votive figurine. Design: Luisa Gloria Mota Velasco.

{ JUNGMIN KIM
WRAPTURE

Reusable gift wrap in various sizes and styles produced for the Wrapture line. Design: Jungmin Kim

PURPOSE: We give gifts to loved ones, family, friends, and others to show appreciation, adoration, respect, or to celebrate a special occasion. Whether the gift is expensive or a small token, we generally enclose it in some fashion, temporarily hiding it from view until the receiver tears into the wrapping, revealing its contents with glee. The wrapping itself can be as beautiful as the thing it is hiding. In the United States, it is common to wrap presents with paper, which, for the most part, is not reusable. I love to save the paper and ribbons from wrapping. Over time, the papers I save become crumpled and messy and in the end I must discard them. Wrapping with cloth is easier than wrapping with paper because it does not need to be cut and it is also more environmentally responsible.

BACK STORY: I got the idea for this project from traditional Korean wrapping cloth, called Bojagi. Bojagi is square-hemmed cloth of various sizes, colors, and designs that Koreans use to wrap, store, or carry things. The origin of Bojagi can be explained in several aspects. First of all Korea has a comparatively cold climate and not rich in natural resources, but it's highly populated. Because of such an environment, the houses were built mostly small and low to the ground, so household articles are designed to take up as little space as possible. The Bojagi are used to wrap almost any kind of item, big or small, and do not take up much space when they are folded to be put away. Other than such space-saving and environmental concerns, there are also some religious factors. Wrapping gifts with Bojagi was a way to express one's respect and affection toward the receiving person.

{ SIERRA KRAUSE
VEGA

PURPOSE: Vega is a line of interior lights that fuse functional lighting and art into one object. Designed to provide versatility, artistic expression, and ambience, each light has the ability to showcase a multitude of interchangeable images, which allows Vega to change and grow with the consumer's style and taste.

BACK STORY: My inspiration to create Vega stems from a passion for both lighting and art for the home. I have always been infatuated with lighting as a general concept. Not only does it provide an important function, but it also has a powerful emotional quality that can induce so many different reactions and moods. A person's home is his or her shelter from the chaos of the outside world, as well as the one place where he or she can truly express himself or herself.

DESIGN: Once the idea for Vega struck, I began spending endless hours scouring the lighting industry to not only see if any similar products existed, but also to get a better feel for materials, types of bulbs and fixtures, and also ways of powering the final product. I looked at materials in which to construct the planes. They had to be stable, heat-resistant, easy to clean, and allow the images to be changed. I looked at several different types of plastic and glass before I settled on Plexiglas. The hardest part of the design process was figuring out how to make the designs interchangeable in an easy and straightforward way. I considered trying to bend the Plexiglass so the designs could slide in, but this weakened the stability of the light. Then I tried using screws, but that meant the consumer would need a drill every time they wanted to change a design. In the end, I decided that magnets were the solution. They were strong enough to hold the design in place and allowed a very simple way for the consumer to change the design of their lamp. In fall 2007, my application for a patent was approved.

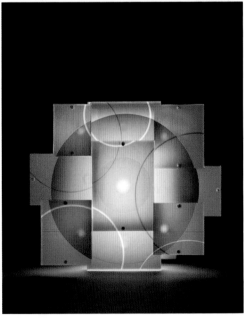

Two styles of lamp for the Vega lighting lines.
Design: Sierra Krause.

{ RICK LANDERS

WINK: WORK AT PLAY

PURPOSE: Wink is a line of office and desktop products intended to bring a little light-hearted joy into the office/work environment, reminding its viewer that life should not be "all work and no play."

BACK STORY: The raison d'êtrè for this project has really come from personal experiences. I love what I do, but I also have a lot of other interests. There have been quite a few times when I have let work get the best of me and have forgotten to take time out for the other important elements in my life. In every job that I have ever had, I've always made it a personal goal to be generally very pleasant around everyone and keep the mood light. Work is hard enough as it is; the last thing any of us really needs is to be around others who make it more difficult or unpleasant. Developing the Wink products gave me an opportunity to really inject some of my personality into everyday, useful objects that anyone would be able to have and make use of around their desks.

DESIGN: The great part about working on 3-D products is that it allowed me to get away from the computer and get my hands dirty. I did a ton of drawing (which up until then I had simply not been doing enough of), and I did a lot of model making using whatever materials I could find. Sometimes it was frustrating not to have the best tools or materials at my disposal, but after a while, I decided to make it part of the fun to figure out how I could make an effective and strong model using materials that I had access to. The process also allowed me to get involved in working and thinking in ways that I had not done before, primarily dealing with the 3-D issue and the abundance of available materials.

From the Wink product line: (Top) "Time Flies" clock, (middle) "Work" clock, and (bottom) "Waste of Time" daily calendar. Design: Rick Landers.

{ ANDY OUTIS
APLY

PURPOSE: Aply are tools for urban cyclists; products that enhance and enable urban cycling by addressing specific problems faced while riding a bicycle in a large city. Most cycling equipment is focused on either recreation or performance (e.g. mountain biking or touring), not on practical need.

BACK STORY: I have been riding bicycles since I was about four years old. When I moved to New York City, I brought my bike along to replace the car that I had used for transportation in California. I quickly found that a bike was my favorite way to get around the city and I ride almost every day for transportation and recreation. Riding a bike in the city is an adventure; dodging taxis, avoiding potholes, and trying to stay alive, all on the way to work, can be both terrifying and exciting. I also found that there were few products offered to help deal with the specific needs of urban cycling.

My dedication to this project was cemented when I attended a Critical Mass bike ride in August 2005 to observe a large group of my target audience and take part in the ride. I was arrested, along with thirty or so other cyclists, for "parading without a permit." My bike was seized and I was held for most of the night in a cell at the 9th Precinct. This was probably the first time an MFAD student was arrested while doing research for a thesis project. While sharing a cell for several hours with fellow cyclists and arrestees, I conducted an impromptu focus group on what they saw as lacking in the current product offerings for urban cycling.

DESIGN: After some experimentation, I developed my own seat cover.

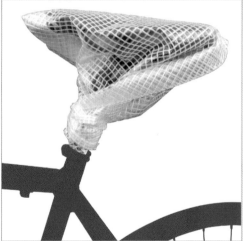

From the Aply bicycle accessories line. (Top) Carrying handle (middle) bike seat and (bottom) seat securer. Design: Andy Outis.

{ JENNIFER PANEPINTO
MESÜ

PURPOSE: To beautifully measure and serve food in the same dish.

BACK STORY: Like many brides-to-be, I wanted to lose weight for my wedding. When I finally spoke to my doctor about what I was doing wrong, I realized that the problem wasn't what I was eating, but the amount of food I was eating. Once I learned this, I started to practice portion control. I began to get rid of the "clean your plate" mentality that I learned at a young age and became more vigilant about measuring and portioning out my meals, so much so, that I began to eat out of a measuring cup. And for a while, I really didn't think anything of it. It just became part of my routine. One night after I came home from school, I was having dinner in my measuring cup and it occurred to me, "Why do I continue to eat out of this measuring cup? I deserve something I can eat out of that doesn't make me feel like I am punishing myself." So I went looking everywhere to find dishes that would measure beautifully, but found nothing. I started working to create something that would not only help me with my lifelong struggle with my weight but would also be an interesting thesis project.

DESIGN: I researched all kinds of plates, dishes, and bowls. Some of the dishes had serving sections that were used as a guide to fill the plate with an approximate amount of food, such as the ones used in the military. I explored this direction but ultimately decided that using a plate or tray like this would just be too cumbersome. The only piece in this exploration that really started to make sense to me was the single bowl. It is the most universal shape and can be used for a variety of things. It was also important that what I made would integrate into the kitchen cabinet along with other dishes. So I started to look at bowls in a set as the most logical form. I tried stacking the

Set of color-coded Mesü stacking bowls for measured portions. Design: Jennifer Panepinto.

bowls, which I thought looked great formally, but I quickly realized that the stack would be too high to fit in most kitchen cabinets and therefore would not be functional. However, the graduated sizes seemed to work. Another challenge was resolving the graphic system so it would be easy to understand what the sizes of the bowls were.

{ KAVITA RAMCHANDRAN
MAYA

Spread from the *Maya* children's book series. Design: Kavita Ramchandran.

PURPOSE: My original thesis began as a book series based on a character I created called Maya. Maya is a five-year-old girl who takes you through different cultural experiences via her journeys across different cities of the world. The purpose was to expose kids at an early age to different cultures in ways that kids can relate to. The philosophy was to help build a comfort and tolerance level to differences in culture at an early age.

BACK STORY: My childhood was spent in Bombay, a cosmopolitan metropolis that is home to fifteen million people in a country of over a billion. India is a country that will very easily overwhelm you with its eighteen official languages, twelve actively represented religious faiths, twenty-eight states of various cultures, foods, sounds, smells and so on. It embodies the very meaning of diversity. As a child, I was constantly exposed to people from all faiths and walks of life. I grew up appreciating and accepting the cultural identities and nuances that differentiate people and make them special in their

own unique way. I grew up reading books of all genres, from *Amar Chitra Kathas* and *Panchatantras* (Indian mythological comics) to *Aesop's Fables*, and *Arabian Nights*, to Marvel comics and Nancy Drew. Sometimes the most important and obvious aspects of our lives are unexamined, especially the way children are influenced by the books they read as they grow up.

DESIGN: For the purpose of my thesis, I envisioned three books: *Maya in Bombay*, *Maya in Beirut*, and *Maya in New York*. I developed *Maya in Bombay* as a full prototype to the series. I entirely created the text and illustrations. The illustrations play a key part in the narrative. In creating my own distinctive visual vocabulary, I incorporated photos of the indigenous vernacular found in the local cultures of each city/cultural experience Maya explores. After I graduated from SVA, the Maya property was extended to other media including animation produced by Nick Jr. (Nickelodeon).

{ AMANDA SPIELMAN

BOOKFOOL

(Left) Bookfool homepage showing selections for books and literary events and (right) logo. Design: Amanda Spielman.

PURPOSE: Bookfool is an online resource for fiction recommendations that matches people to books based on factors such as mood, personal circumstances, and geographical locations of interest. Unlike sites such as Amazon that suggest books based on purchasing history or an "if you like X, you'll like Y" algorithm, Bookfool knows and loves novels and makes informed recommendations much like a bookseller in an independent bookstore.

BACK STORY: I have always loved books and I have always loved to read. I'm the kind of person who inhales the scent of a book before reading it. Growing up, the library was my second home. My younger brother, on the other hand, didn't read anything he wasn't forced

to. It killed me that he was missing out on something so important to me and finally, when he was 14, I made a very calculated recommendation, *The Hitchhiker's Guide to the Galaxy* by Douglas Adams. My brother has been reading like a fiend ever since. Bookfool is founded on the belief that more of these connections will encourage people to read and offer them more satisfying reading experiences.

DESIGN: I kept an eye on the design of other book sites while I was designing Bookfool. I wanted the site to stand apart from the competition while still feeling that it was of and about books.

{ SUNNIVA DJUPEDAL DE VILLIERS

THE SUNNIVA COLLECTION

PURPOSE: The Sunniva Collection is a line of dinnerware aimed at using design to shift the perception of people with disabilities from people who are disabled to people who are enabled. The products celebrate aesthetics as being equal to function and challenge our assumptions of what is normal. They question why people with disabilities are only offered products designed to look as "normal" as possible but without any aesthetic consideration. The Sunniva Collection brings dynamic, flowing lines to the table and improves your dining experience through the Valmue plate, the Kala cup, the Vivendel 1 flatware, and the Vivendel 2 dining utensil.

BACK STORY: I was born with a malformed left hand and have several times encountered the lack of aesthetic consideration within the world of products for people with disabilities. Personally, I didn't need many products to help me while I was growing up but I did need a good knife when dining. My father and I developed a silver knife that perfectly fit my hand and allowed me to easily cut food on the plate. The Sunniva Collection is a further development of this knife, extending the concept to a complete set of flatware, cups, and plates. It is crucial to understand that every person with a disability is different, not because of the disability, but because every human being has a different mindset. What each person finds helpful is very personal, and is therefore often ignored when designing for disabilities. Customization when designing for this audience is an important step.

DESIGN: The design was conceived after looking at organic shapes in nature and the human body. Together with my mother, who is a ceramic artist, we created the porcelain designs for the Kala Cup and Valmue Plate.

The Sunniva dinnerwear collection: (Top) Fork, (middle left) Knife, (middle right) Kala cup, (bottom) Valmue plat. Design: Sunniva Djupedal De Villiers; production of cup and plate: Turid Haye Studio, Norway

The brand was established through the development of the name, logo, tone of voice, visual look, brand placement, and so forth. I wanted the brand to have a personal tone, to tell the story of the designer behind the products, and this very much guided the logo, name, and final look.

{ JESSE WILLMON

COMMIX (WWW.COM-MIX.ORG)

Homepage from com-mix.org featuring character and style options. Design: Jesse Willmon.

PURPOSE: Commix is an online tool for creating your own comics. It allows participants to use art from some of today's top comic artists to make unique ideas come to life. Users arrange the art, write their own copy, and choose the layout for their comic. Beyond this, com-mix.org is a community of people that can edit each other's comments and have conversations on the site about their comics. It also allows people who don't think they have the drawing ability to make comics to express their ideas.

BACK STORY: I was a Web designer by trade, but I always loved comics. I wanted to find a way to combine what I was good at with what I loved, and this is what I came up with. The real back story is I wanted a reason to hang out with some of the artists. I guess I'm a fan boy at heart and really just nerd out about getting to hang out with people I admire.

DESIGN: The design style that I chose was made to look easy. The idea of making your own comics like this was fairly new, and if it looked computer generated and technological, then people would think it was complex. So by making it all hand drawn and relaxed, it actually made people more comfortable with the process. I also wanted to stick as close to how actual comics are made as I could. So when it came to designing the site, I actually drew out by hand how every page would look and scanned it in. From there, the whole thing was colored and rearranged slightly.

{ CELIA SIN-TIEN CHENG

CRAVINGS

PURPOSE: Cravings is an online guide to New York City eateries. It judges specific dishes rather than the restaurant as a whole. Every good restaurant has one or two superior dishes on the menu; Cravings strives to identify those dishes and recommend them. The site introduces readers to the best foods, wines, and events in the city. There are also occasional travel pieces that recommend good eats in other cities and countries.

BACK STORY: Everyone has a passion or interest; mine happens to be food. I wake up with food cravings and find that if I don't satiate them, they don't go away. When I get together with friends, we start our conversations about food, and if we ever manage to stray from the topic, we always come back to it. During a meal, I am already planning what I will be eating at the next meal. I am a discerning eater and extremely critical of the quality of food. When I judge food, it is based on taste, texture, composition, and satisfaction in all aspects. As a result, I have become a source of restaurant guidance to many friends. When approached for restaurant recommendations, I always start by asking, "What are you craving?" Over time, I realized that for me to reach out and aid a larger audience, it would be more efficient and helpful to create a systematic guide.

DESIGN: Cravings is the culmination of my passion for all things gastronomic, so I wanted all sections of the site to be extensions of the central theme of cravings, hence the naming conventions of sections like Tasting, Craving, Indulging, Happening and Sipping. In addition to the photographs on the site, the colors constantly change as new features are added, which is the most important design element because it refreshes the site and gives it a sense of depth. My love for colors and my innate need to feel and translate the subjects I write about have led me to continuously change the color palette of the site in fun, delicious, and appropriate ways.

Feature and Events pages from Cravings, an online guide to New York City eateries (findyourcraving.com). Design: Celia Sin-Tien Cheng

{ JEFFREY EVERETT

EL JEFE DESIGN (WWW.ELJEFEDESIGN.COM)

PURPOSE: I believe that the T-shirt is the best way to express one's individuality and that if I can convince one person to buy a shirt I have done something right.

BACK STORY: I originally started my company (under a different name) for my School of Visual Arts thesis. I didn't want to change the entire block, city, or world; I just wanted to reach the individual person.

DEVELOPMENT: I had to learn to legally protect myself, to do inventory, and to calculate prices. I had to learn that a design business is not all about the design, but more about the business; a product won't sell itself.

(Left) El Jefe Design promotional posters and (right) logo. Design: Jeffrey Everett.

DESIGN: One of the descriptions I frequently receive for my designs is "cute and evil," as exemplified by the Heart Skull shirt as a signature example. I take everyday things and twist them just a bit to make them unique and interesting, such as doing a shirt with a royal looking crest. A lot of companies have done them, but I try to use animals such as dodo birds and asses instead of lions and hawks. I like it when people take a second look at my shirts and grin.

CHAPTER 2

FROM IDEA TO
PRODUCT

You may have a great idea but it will remain just an idea unless you commit to taking the next steps to ensure that it gets into the marketplace. After all, you know this product better than anyone else. You are the best advocate for its viability. So take a breath, survey the options, and make a concerted effort to promote it to prospective investors or customers.

As an entrepreneur, you must be able to convey the breadth and depth of your individual product or product line, who your target audience is, how you will reach this audience, and why your creation is better than that of any of your competitors. Therefore, it is essential to know what your competition (if any) is doing so that you can highlight the key differences that make your product unique. The following are steps you must follow (sometimes not in this order).

THE SELL

It is necessary to determine how to position your product, how to price it, and how to package it. Define a sales strategy and the various distribution channels that will reach your audience.

Start by identifying your target customer and developing a strategy to convey that your product is meeting their needs. That means you have to understand the competition so that you can show why your product is better. Focus on the differences that make your product superior. List the characteristics that make your product stand out from all similar products on the market and highlight this in all your promotional materials.

Create, conduct, and analyze a market research survey to understand and communicate with your target audience. This research will help you to find out more about what the end user wants and build a strategy.

MARKET SURVEYS

Do an online market survey and test your intended audience so that you can confirm the assumption you have been making all along about who needs this product and how much they are willing to spend for it. This type of research  and analysis is really valuable and should not be overlooked; it's how you define the customer on which you will focus all your marketing efforts. It will also confirm that you are on track. You can find answers to a lot of questions, such as the spending habits, age, income level, and need of the potential customer. It will also provide other important data on lifestyles, enabling you to develop a strategy for your product's price point, promotion, and placement. The great benefit of knowing all this information up front is increasing your profit potential and minimizing your risk

There are many online surveys that are available to help you do the market research. Some offer basic, scaled-down versions for free, while others allow you to customize surveys for a nominal monthly fee in order to get as much feedback as you want about your customer's likes and dislikes. When developing a survey, be sure to start off with a concrete strategy and know what it is you want to find out. It can be an effective tool. Here are some model surveys:

- www.questionpro.com
- www.surveymonkey.com
- info.zoomerang.com

BUSINESS PLAN

Whether your idea is a finished product, a prototype, or a concept that you want to sell to an investor, you will have to develop a business plan. Even if you are going to market the product on your own, you will still need a business plan; it's the foundation for your success. It will take a little time to do, but it forces you to think in a systematic way. And the research and thinking you put into it will help you develop a strategy for every aspect of bringing this product to market and hopefully avoid mistakes along the way. At the very least, it will help you determine the unit cost, which has to take into account every dollar that went into making the product, including shipping, materials, labor, packaging, overhead, and so on. You can only determine an accurate selling price for your product if you have correctly calculated your unit cost. Determining the price point will require some strategy. You have to tally all of your costs to ensure that you won't lose money, but you must also not price yourself out of the market. Do your research so that the price is attractive to the customer but generates enough profit for you.

Whether your idea is a finished product, a prototype, or a concept that you want to sell to an investor, you will have to develop a business plan.

There are many volunteer organizations that will provide counselors to assist you with your business plan or give you free business advice and tools. Here are some model plans:

- www.score.org
- www.entrepreneur.com

PROMOTION

Promotion for your product starts at the very beginning with the packaging, point of purchase displays, and anything else you can do to grab your customer's attention and encourage them to buy your product. The objective is to get out information about your product. Determine what your objective is and then develop both a short- and long-term promotional plan to help position your product and increase sales.

THE BRAND

This is a more complex issue than simply developing a logo, and one that may not be as necessary in the early stages of marketing your product as in the late stages. But from the outset, it is important to create a viable name (not something that merely sounds good, but has no relation to the product function or goal), then develop an identity (and even an identity system). This is currently called the brand, but in truth it is more fundamental. Every product needs to have a mnemonic attached to it that distinguishs its virtues but also locates it

in the marketplace. Design these attributes well (they can always be changed once the product is sold), but put your best—and smartest—foot forward.

DISTRIBUTION

Find a distribution partner if you are unable to get your product to the customer on your own. There are many established distribution channels (a middle person or company that will get your product to the intended audience), but you have to figure out which partner best suits your needs.

You may decide to sell your product directly, via mail order or on the Internet. If you plan to sell your product yourself on the Web, make sure you are registered with search engines and that you are linked with other similar or related Web pages.

THE PITCH

Like throwing a baseball over home plate, the entrepreneur must throw strikes, too. It takes skill and confidence, but in the end it's the idea that makes the difference. So, how do you pitch an idea? Here are three ways:

1. Be self-confident when talking to potential collaborators, interested investors, or buyers. You know more about this product that anyone else, and that should come across.
2. Describe your product and for whom it is designed in a concise manner. Include

There is no longer a legal requirement to identify a work as being copyrighted. However, the copyright symbol or other form of copyright notice gives notice to the world that the work is yours and that it is protected under copyright law.

the narrative behind the product, such as intent or philosophy and if there is any cultural relevance. The goal is to clarify what your product is and convince someone that it is viable.

3. It's important to discuss the nature of the competition, so that you can say why your product is unique or better than anything else on the market. You should also show how you intend to reach your audience.

Once you've pitched the idea, be prepared to talk about the following issues:

- Convey how your product works and why it is important to your intended audience. Talk a little about how you will fabricate and market your product during the short and long term.
- Pitch visuals including your design scheme. These are as important as words. Include your logo, package designs, charts, graphs, and anything else that illustrates your concept.

PROTECT YOUR INTELLECTUAL PROPERTY

Now that you have conceived a product, don't let anyone steal your intellectual property. In order to maintain ownership of your creative work or product, you'll have to make some choices about licensing versus

selling and how to negotiate with clients and vendors.

Frank Martinez, attorney and esteemed faculty member in the SVA MFA Designer as Author program, gives the following overview on how to protect your work.

The Copyright Act allows you to seek the additional protections offered as an incentive to formal registration. Under U.S. law, a federal copyright technically exists when the work is created and fixed in a tangible medium. Since digital works are, by their very nature, fleeting, the "fixation" of digital works is deemed to occur when it is capable of being viewed or "fixed" in computer code. Ideas cannot be copyrighted; reducing the creative concept to a tangible form is always required to register any creative work. Publication is no longer required prior to copywriting, but unpublished works have a different status under copyright law and care should be taken when registering a copyright for unpublished works so as to ensure that such a registration fits into your plans.

U.S. copyright law does not limit the grant of a copyright to U.S. citizens only. Foreign nationals and foreign corporations are also entitled to register a copyright in the United States. However, since the term "author "and the work-for-hire doctrine play an important role under U.S. laws, a foreign national or foreign corporation seeking to register a copyright should understand the terms and their usage under U.S. copyright law.

There is no longer a legal requirement to identify a work as being copyrighted. However, the copyright symbol or other form of copyright notice gives notice to the world that the work is yours and that it is protected under copyright law. There are several generally accepted forms of copyright notice. At a minimum, the "*c* in a circle" should be used.

- © COPYRIGHT (YEAR) (NAME) ALL RIGHTS RESERVED.
- © COPYRIGHT (YEAR)
- ©

Among the additional rights granted by a formal registration are the possibility of enhanced or "statutory damages" of up to $150,000 per infringement and the recovery of attorney's fees. Since the official filing fee is a mere $45, the cost of peace of mind is truly one of the last bargains offered by the U.S. government. In addition, it is possible to register a collection of similar works, reducing your costs even further. While requiring additional care, such registrations are quite useful to the designer on a budget.

In a perfect world, any creative work would be registered within three months of publication or offering for sale, which also includes the display of prototypes or mockups shown for the purpose of building commercial interest. However, an application for the registration of a creative work will be accepted at just about any time. Lawsuits related to the infringement of works that are registered after an infringement occurs are usually not eligible for a claim of statutory damages. If you are unsure as to your rights, the U.S. Copyright Office publishes many helpful information circulars, most of which are available online. However, the use of a copyright expert or attorney is wise when dealing with complex legal questions or weighty business endeavors involving copyright or other forms of intellectual property. Here are some helpful websites:

- www.copyright.gov
- www.uspto.gov/main/patents.htm
- www.uspto.gov/go/oeip/catalog/ products/pp-a2n-1.htm

THE BEGINNING

Even after following these procedures, there is more to do, but this will give you the optimum start. In the following chapter you'll read about the experiences of a wide range of design entrepreneurs. Each has gone about the process differently, but in pursuit of a common goal they have addressed all these components. In the final analysis, as an entrepreneur you are inventing not only the product, but the means of getting it accepted, often through a combination of conventional and novel approaches and good luck.

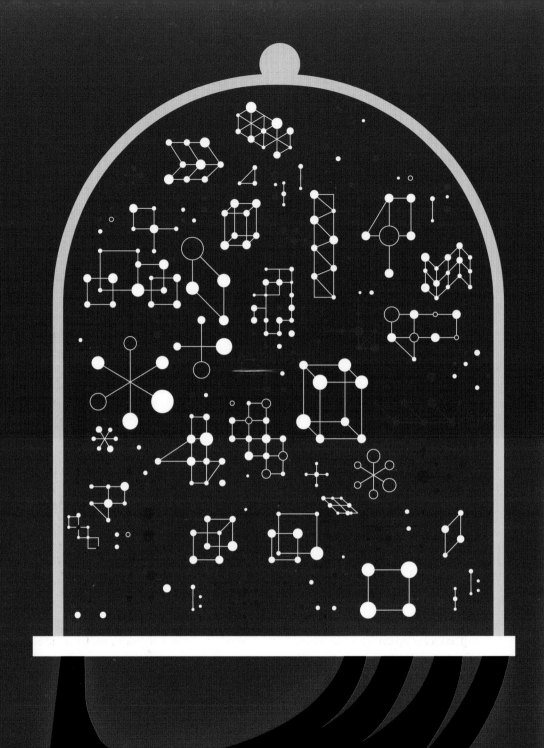

CHAPTER 3

CATALOGING IDEAS:
VIABLE PRODUCTS BY DESIGNERS

There are as many different kinds of design entrepreneurs as there are nondesign entrepreneurs and as many ways of practicing entrepreneurship as there are entrepreneurial business models. Becoming a design entrepreneur does not require following a strict paradigm, yet it does demand marshaling one's design skills, talents, and passions—whatever they are—to conceive the idea and then make it whole.

Of course, the design entrepreneur has a leg up on the nondesigner because the means of visualizing and fabricating are in one person (and two hands). But even so, once the idea is realized, the design entrepreneur need not follow through on all the necessary production, promotion, and marketing components of the project. Sometimes the entrepreneur will launch a business to support all aspects of the project, while other times the best strategy is to license or even sell it outright to an existing business, like a publisher, distributor, or manufacturer better able to produce and market the wares. Therefore, imposing a standard operating procedure on design entrepreneurs would be a huge mistake and is avoided here.

What is so liberating about entrepreneurship in general, and design entrepreneurship in particular, is that anything is possible as long as the individual or collaborative team have the gumption to bring the products to the marketplace, through whatever means are possible. While one becomes an entrepreneur to control the destiny of one's ideas, this can be done through ownership or selling the entire scheme to a third party. Either way is fine.

The dictionary definition of an entrepreneur is one who starts a new business "in response to identified opportunities." But the misconception about design entrepreneurship is that the business is an end in itself. Not all design entrepreneurs will develop a business entity with a self-perpetuating infrastructure. Not all design entrepreneurs have the intestinal fortitude to build large businesses, for which design and business are inseparable. For many, if not most, the one-off product is enough to satisfy the entrepreneurial urge—to sell ideas and products through existing companies, from which they may receive a percentage of the sales in the form of a royalty. Does this make them any less entrepreneurial than those who start and manage their own businesses? The simple answer is no!

In fact, by following this practice, they avoid some of the issues inherent in being a small business owner. Some designers prefer the simplicity of only working in the "creative vacuum," while others keenly understand that creation is, in and of itself, not enough. Some designers just want to make things that will hopefully reach an audience through an ad hoc manner. Others have partners in which one person runs the business side while the other provides the creative output.

Of course, not all entrepreneurial projects radically alter a designer's life or livelihood. Many of the design entrepreneurs featured here run their own design studios and produce their products on the side, but within the traditional business model of their design firm.

The World Wide Web has certainly become a wellspring for new and old businesses and for all kinds of entrepreneurs in that it not only created a new avenue for selling and publishing their wares, but it has expanded the businesses, taking them in unexpected directions.

For some designers, profit is relative (and not always translated into dollars and cents). Many view their profit as coming from the nexus of art, design, and commerce. While no less entrepreneurial in spirit (and deed), their products are defined for them as art rather than commodity, yet when the art is sold, it becomes a commodity. While a true purist defines art in a narrow way, there are also fungible boundaries. The boundary between one-of-a-kind art and multiples (that have value as commodities) is quickly redefining the art market as well as the design field.

Designers, by definition, routinely seek out the "next thing," if not the next "big" thing. If it means combining art and design, or fashion and graphics or any other mix of media and talents, they'll do it. The need to find the new is what generates all entrepreneurial spirit and makes it such a challenging field.

The following case studies have one thing in common (aside from the obvious fact that some share the same basic media—books, periodicals, cards, T-shirts, type fonts, and so on): Each tells a story about the unique inventions of design creators who have attempted, with varying degrees of success, to find large and small audiences for their respective wares. Each saw either a personal (i.e., autobiographical), social, cultural, or consumer need and invented a product to fill it. The range is as impressive as the quality of the inventions. And the stories of how they got to where they are offer many models for future design entrepreneurs.

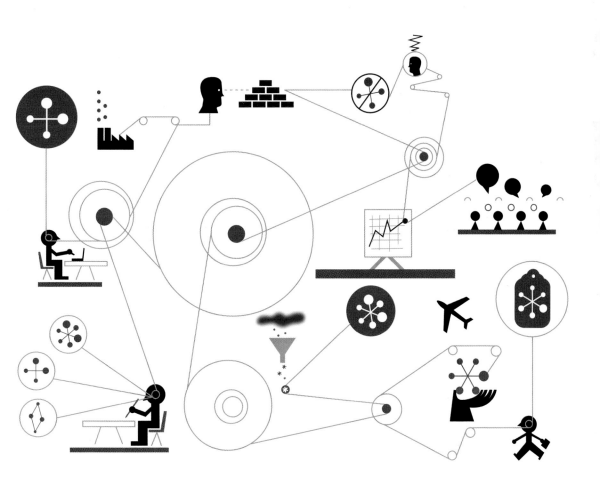

{ CHARLES SPENCER ANDERSON

POP INK

Charles S. Anderson established his packaging, identity, interactive, advertising, and product design firm in 1989. Since then, he has produced graphic identities for clients that include French Paper, Levi's, Target, Williams-Sonoma, Sony, Paramount Pictures, the New York Times, *and Nike. CSA Archive repurposes and licenses vintage graphics for contemporary use. Pop Ink, a development company, packages and publishes books and related products.*

CSA Design is a thriving design studio. How much of your business is now divided between CSA Archive and Pop Ink?

An approximate breakdown would be one-third design projects for clients including French Paper Company, one-third CSA Images, and one-third Pop Ink product development.

You've long been involved with "vernacular" art and design to the point that your early style was built on it. How much of your design today draws upon the materials you've accumulated and now have funneled into Pop Ink?

Much of our work still has its roots in the vernacular, but is mostly used as a starting point to develop new, more modern images that express new ideas.

How do you find the material you use in books such as *Love Sick*, *Happy Kitty Bunny Pony*, **and** *Goth-icky*?

I have spent a disproportionately large percentage of my life (since 1974) searching for images around the world and also purchasing collections of original artwork along with the original and commissioned art and photographs that we have created over the past 30 years.

Do you think of this as nostalgia or something else?

I think it has nothing to do with nostalgia and more to do with a love of great art, or even art that's so bad it's amazing someone could actually come up with it. We call this "crapstock," and I have been compiling a file of this for many years.

Sounds like it's about harvesting pop culture and in the case of the plates, napkins, gift wrap, and soaps, making a new consumer vocabulary. Would you agree?

"Harvesting" is too pleasant a notion. Tibor [Kalman] once described it as "strip mining the past," but it's actually more like tunnel mining—a difficult, time-consuming, sometimes dirty job that requires digging and sifting through tons and tons of rubble to find a single rough gem and then cutting, shaping, and polishing it to perfection to transform it into something worthwhile.

Plates have become rather popular in the past year. What made you get involved with them?

My love of all things plastic, especially melamine—the perfect durable, futuristic material designed to never degrade and to be impervious to nearly anything you can throw at it. It's also fade-proof, nearly indestructible, and a

Gift Wrap made from clip art and unique decorative elements.
Design: Charles Spencer Anderson Design/Pop Ink.

Decorative plate set with prosaic woodland scenes. Design:
Charles Spencer Anderson Design/Pop Ink.

perfect surface for art, culinary art, as we call it. I have
a collection of over 100,000 pieces of plastic junk, the
basis of the CSA Plastock photo archive.

**How difficult was it for you to develop this
business? What was the business model you
adopted to turn this into a profitable concern?**
Very difficult. I have been developing products since
1983—first with posters, watches, plastic can-o-junk,
magnetic personalities, pens, apparel, pins, Slacks
cologne, and now Pop Ink soaps, plates, gift wrap, note
cards, and books. There was no business plan, or real
business model, and always more concern about the
production of unique and well-designed products than
profits. I guess, from that perspective, we have been
wildly successful to have not gone out of business and
to be able to afford to try again and again, learning
more each time.

**Did you ever imagine that you would be doing this
entrepreneurial pursuit for so long? Likewise, could
you predict that it would be so successful?**
I had no idea it would take this long to start to develop
something that is just now beginning to work.

How is the Pop Ink line doing?
Its doing better than any of our previous attempts (but
that's not saying much.) It's about one year since our full
catalog launched and we've seen some pretty big sales in
2007, including interest overseas. It's too soon to say, but
it seems to be finally working this time around.

**With Pop Ink, you've veered away from the CSA
Archive of licensing materials. What do you see in
your five-year future?**
Pop Ink is a licensed brand. French Paper is the
manufacturer. They assemble, collate, pack, ship, and
carry inventory. We get a royalty on all sales for designing
and overseeing the production of the products. I prefer
to deal in both the actual (tangible) products and digital
(intangible) products. Each side helps the other, although
the warehousing and shipping of the digital images
worldwide is much easier. In five years, we'll hopefully
continue to expand the product selection and continue to
design saccharine sweet, slightly disturbing, but strangely
compelling art and artifacts for a postmodern world.

(Top) Soap Box Packaging using vintage pulp illustrations, and (bottom) *Goth-Icky* Book. Design: Charles Spencer Anderson Design/Pop Ink.

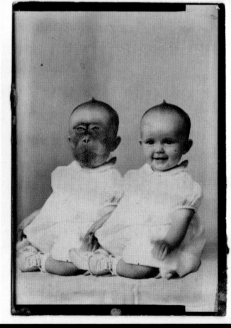

(Top) Front and back cover images from the CD *Cobalt Blue: True Stories about the Art Worltd*, written and performed by Marshall Arisman and (bottom) spreads from the book *Divine Elvis*.

{ MARSHALL ARISMAN

COLBALT BLUE

M arshall Arisman's paintings and drawings are in the permanent collection of the Brooklyn Museum, the National Museum of American Art, and the Smithsonian Institution, as well as private and corporate collections. He is the Chair of the MFA Illustration program at the School of Visual Arts in New York and is the subject of a full-length documentary film directed by Tony Silver titled, Facing the Audience: The Arts of Marshall Arisman.

You've been an illustrator and painter for decades. When did you first begin doing entrepreneurial things?

My intent when I was attending Pratt Institute (1956–1960) was to be a graphic designer. After graduation, I worked for General Motors in the experimental graphic division. Three months later, I realized that I hated working with people and solving other people's problems. That drove me to freelance illustrating and the beginning of thinking about myself as an entrepreneur. My intent at this point was not managing a business undertaking but to explore the various components of myself through art. I was twenty-five at this point, and like many artists, I was window-shopping for a direction that reflected me. I found not one direction but many.

Cobalt Blue was your first attempt at combining your remarkable gifts with the spoken word to an audio medium. How did you plunge into this?

I like stories. The best ones are, of course, true. I also like to play the saxophone. I called Chuck Hammer, an old friend and monster guitar player who now composes music for the Discovery Channel, and asked him if he was bored. He said he was. I told stories. Chuck laid in a soundtrack and I packaged it.

Did you sell Cobalt Blue? And if not, what was your objective?

Printed Matter, a wonderful source for offbeat books, sold some copies and I sold some on my website, but I gave away the majority. There were two objectives in doing Cobalt Blue: one was fun; the other was to add a soundtrack to the paintings I do. There is so much pretentious artspeak out there that I thought it might be refreshing to simply track the stories that surround the art. Unfortunately, critics and art historians write most of the language that defines artwork. Artists, in turn, mimic the language.

The Divine Elvis is a book, but it's also something else. What is the story behind creating this entity, and what is your goal in doing it?

The goal for writing a full-length, illustrated novel was to find out if I could sustain a story for more than one page. I like the process and time I spend writing. Writing activates a curious stream of consciousness inside me that is different than painting. Writing occurs after the painting and not before it.

I spent two years painting monkeys, not your run-of-the-mill monkeys, but sacred monkeys. Monkeys, in my opinion, carry knowledge, as do various other animals. Saturated in "monkeydom," I thought it would

be amazing to write a coming-of-age story about a boy named Marshall who was born with a twin brother that was a monkey. I have a brother two years older than me. In the book, he is from another planet. My mother was a twin with six sets of twins in her family. My grandmother on my father's side was a noted psychic and Spiritualist minister. My mother's parents were Pentecostal Holy Rollers. I knew enough family secrets that I could betray them in writing now that my parents are dead. Initially, *The Divine Elvis* was only in written form. Then I added over 100 illustrations. If all goes according to plan, Excelsior Publishing (they publish *EXILE: The Literary*

Quarterly) will publish the book in Canada. Then the movie, and the *big* money will roll in.

You also produced a newspaper that combines your art and others' in odd commentaries. Was this designed to turn into a business?
Brief Encounter with Some Very Fine Artists preceded the illustrated novel. Looking back, the newspaper was my first attempt at combining words and images. Once again, the goal was not to make money but to poke fun at the art world. I was born in upstate New York in a town surrounded by trailers. For those of us lucky enough to live in houses,

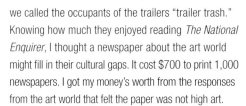

(Left) *Cat Be Bop*, a children's book about a jazzy feline and his catty fans.

(Above) Illustration from *Brief Encounter with Some Very Fine Artists* by Arisman.

If the sky were always blue, what would your wish be for how this work plays on the world's stage?
The audience for what I do is limited; some would say "slow." I am a bad barometer for what will sell or for what is appealing to my fellow man. The people who fish in their pockets for hard cash to buy anything I do are always surprising but never mainstream. If all of this were to play on a world stage, I would expect no more than a handful of people to show up. In our high-powered world of buying and selling, that would be more than enough.

At the end of the day, are you an artist or an artist entrepreneur?
I am an artist looking for outlets for what I do. The printed page, the gallery wall, an illustrated book, or short films are entrepreneurial, but they are also simply extensions of my expression.

we called the occupants of the trailers "trailer trash." Knowing how much they enjoyed reading *The National Enquirer*, I thought a newspaper about the art world might fill in their cultural gaps. It cost $700 to print 1,000 newspapers. I got my money's worth from the responses from the art world that felt the paper was not high art.

Do you even have a business plan when you go out on these creative limbs?
In my case, starting with a business plan is simply bad business.

Surrealist

black — glasses

−red lips / red lip earrings

−Platnium white hair pulled back tight w/ bottom dipped in red

−one piece body suit with hands appliqued on nude sheer

−gloves seperate or part of body suit

−plain black high pumps patent / red heels?

EVE KITTEN

Surrealist-inspired sketch of Eve Kitten, a sensual feline figure designed by Nancy Bacich; photo: Wing Cheung.

{ NANCY BACICH

EVE KITTEN

Nancy Bacich has been designing luxury handbags for the past twelve years. Her collections are sold at high-end retail stores such as Sak's Fifth Avenue and Bergdorf Goodman. Four years ago, she created Eve Kitten, a character that was developed into a promotional lipstick color by MAC Cosmetics, an art exhibition in New York City, a doll that is a "must have" item, and a chocolate bar.

How did you come up with the idea for Eve Kitten, and how did you bring it to life as a brand?

I have been drawing Eve my whole life as a fashion designer. My brother Christopher and I decided one summer to combine our different drawing styles and Gotham's lingerie super hero Eve Kitten was born. In April 2005, I partnered with my friend Patrick McDonald, who organized the first art exhibit at Gallagher's Art and Fashion Gallery. The Eve Kitten exhibit was a natural follow up to the previous show on Edie Sedgwick.

Eve Kitten has become quite the brand with dolls and chocolates. How did you get it onto so many platforms?

We had a big vision for the exhibit and realized we needed sponsorship. With the portfolio of drawings we met James Gager, the creative director of MAC Cosmetics, at their corporate headquarters. Within moments, he green-lighted the project. A well-known industry visionary, James provided us with the support and talent to produce the artwork in oversized, mixed media canvases and cast large, custom metal push pins for installation. MAC artists' bodypainted a model as the "surrealist" Eve Kitten, a special gift lipstick was created for the guests, and pink champagne was popped. The gallery floor was painted pink—Eve's favorite color! The first Eve Kitten show was a great success.

How did you finance this? Do you have backers or is it your own investment?

Financing came two ways, through sponsorship and licensing. Eve's debut was such a success, MAC sponsored "Eve Kitten Hollywood" and "The World of Eve Kitten" in 2005 and 2006, respectively. The "World of Eve Kitten" at the new Patricia Field's Bowery boutique in New York City introduced an Eve Kitten doll and an exotic chocolate bar. Jason Wu of Integrity Toys produced the doll and Fritz Knipschildt produced the chocolate bar, both through licensing arrangements. The limited-edition, stitched comic book was self-published.

Three exotic flavors of Eve Kitten chocolate bars produced by Fritz Knipschildt; photo: Cheung.

Working Phase

(Left) Eve Kitten Comics, the impetus for the line designed by Nancy Bacich and her brother Christopher Bacich; photos: Wing Cheung.

(Below) Eve Kitten Dolls in various sexy outfits.

What did you have to learn and know that you didn't know or learn before?

As a sole proprietor of a luxury handbag collection for more than twelve years, I felt the need to explore other artistic avenues. So instead of going to China to get lower prices for expanded commercial distribution, I went the opposite way—back to the drawing board.

Do you work on this alone?

The remarkable difference is that Eve Kitten is not a solo project; it's a team. The constant team is myself as the creator and artist, Christopher as the writer and cocreator, and Patrick as the media marketing man. Our philosophy of Eve Kitten is to constantly keep it moving forward with art exhibits, storylines, and additional artistic collaborations. Recently, we had an afternoon tea at The National Arts Club in Gramercy Park. Other collaborations have included graffiti artists Stash and Sharp providing authentic touches, poet Harry Koutoukas composing Eve's quote, "We are all kittens caught in the yarn of life," DJ and rock-and-roll singer Keanan Duffty creating the "Meow Mix," and Stephen Knoll, the Madison Avenue hairdresser, who created the hair for the first doll.

How successful is Eve in the marketplace?

Patricia Field, award-winning costume designer from *Sex in the City*, anointed the Eve Kitten doll the "must have" on a luxury Japanese retailer's website. This caused a lot of blogging and led to a complete sellout!

And who is your audience?

Truthfully, the Eve Kitten market is unfolding to us, but the great news is that Eve Kitten is as appealing to men as much as women.

Have you had to alter the character to fit the market response?

Not one bit.

Has this become your total job and focus?

That would be my dream.

After four years doing this, what is your next four-year plan?

We would love to do an animated feature, a lingerie collection, a book, and more collaboration with other artists.

Does Eve Kitten have, well, a life of its own now?

Oh yes. It's been a relief to me that I no longer must explain who she is—she has become a noun. We are now marketing Eve Kitten to the art, media, and fashion world in Japan.

"La Dolce Eve" doll, the sexy vamp designed to make Ken dolls go wild designed by Bacich; photo: Katy Winn.

{ YVES BEHAR

FUSEPROJECT

Yves Behar is an industrial designer and artist whose fuseproject studio's philosophy is rooted in the idea that intelligent and consistent stories can be developed for their clients and their products. His diverse work spans products, environments, packaging, fashion, graphics, and strategy for clients such as Herman Miller, Swarovski, and Hewlett-Packard. Behar has been the subject of a solo show at the Museum of Modern Art in San Francisco, California.

For a long time you have produced entrepreneurially. How much of your practice is entrepreneurial versus client-driven?

Fuseproject is increasingly entrepreneurial. About 50 percent of our projects have a mixture of equity, royalty, fees, and profit sharing, depending on what makes sense. Fuseproject is focused on three types of projects:

1. Creative partnerships with small-and large-sized companies on new products and new brands.
2. Civic projects that apply design to important causes such as education (One Laptop Per Child) or health (NYC Condom AIDS prevention).
3. Cultural projects for which we work with museums, galleries, and companies that are patrons of experimental projects.

How do you manage and market your entrepreneurial wares? Do you seek out backers and producers or do you finance your endeavors on your own?

We always work as outside entrepreneurs, building together game-changing companies.

Aliph Jawbone Bluetooth Headset is a perfect high-tech fashion accessory. Designer: Yves Behar/ fuseproject.

How was Jawbone conceived?

We met with the founders when they were a start-up backed by large voice communication (VC) companies. When the founders decided to restart the effort and exit the VC firm, we went underground with them and developed the current products and company over two years of intense work. Our new position for the company is a premium voice communication company combining the best technology with an approach that makes the product and brand a personal face accessory, recognizing that what people put on their face should be branded and designed more like jewelry than techno gizmo.

What was the process of developing the perfect form for the ultimate function?

The process meant a lot of partnering with engineers and manufacturers and a lot of intervention by the creative team at the business level.

What has been the outcome? Success or otherwise?

Jawbone is our most successful partnership to date, as it is both critically and commercially successful. It's the highest-rated cell phone product on CNET ever and the best selling headset with large providers, such as AT&T and Apple.

Design is the glue that can solve problems, create opportunities, and shape both strategy and execution.

The company is very profitable, growing rapidly, and we are building many more products. Jawbone has been backed by Silicon Valley's heavyweights, who believe in its unique positioning. The icing on the cake is that we launched it with the iPhone in 157 Apple stores.

Can you describe the conceptual thinking behind the Leaf Light?

Leaf was commissioned by Herman Miller, but soon became a very personal project for me. It took over four years to design and then create the LED technology to complete Leaf. It is rare to be able to design both the light source and the light. Additionally, Leaf is the first product of a new lighting business for Herman Miller and the first residential, as well as contract, product in many years for the company. We recently launched the second light project for Herman Miller called Ardea.

The central idea of Leaf is to bring the option of shifting the light from a soft, mood-enhancing, warm glow to an efficient, bright, cool-colored light. I wanted Leaf to be both futuristic and familiar, like a blade of grass that lights up at night. At the same time, a new technology demands a new expression and a new function—the ability to change the light from cold to warm, focusing on the experience of the light. The simplicity of the form does enhance the experience; the emotion of the light touches you, while one can actually touch the product.

Environmentally speaking, Leaf's sculptural form was created to minimize material use and mechanical complexities while maximizing light options. It's LEDs carry a 60,000-hour lifespan at full power and cut energy use by 40 percent when compared with a compact fluorescent light bulb.

Do you follow any particular business model or does each project trigger its own process?

There are some principles we believe in that apply to all the projects and need to be agreed upon with our partners:

1. Design is not an ingredient. I believe design is at the center of business strategy and at the center of business execution. Design is the glue that can solve problems, create opportunities, and shape both strategy and execution. So design is fully integrated into all of the aspects of the venture. For example, on Jawbone, we not only established the principles behind the brand and customer experience, we also drove the execution of the packaging, the out of the box experience, and, website.

2. Design is an escape from the commodity trap. Design, whether brand design or product design, enables companies to sell experience, not commodity. Think about the difference between $0.01 per cup for bulk-priced coffee beans and $5 for a Starbucks product. Design also creates a first-player advantage and defensible connections with consumers.

3. Design drives differentiation. To battle commoditization and competition, design gives the consumer something distinct in a sea of sameness and creates or leverages specific advantages unique to the brand. The key is to have the vision and the guts to be a "game-changing" company.

The Herman Miller Leaf Lamp alters the way illumination is perceived. Designer: Behar/fuseproject.

PLAZM

28

PLAZM 28 $10 US / $12 CDN

2 8>

0 74470 81311 8

Milton Glaser

Plazm magazine, issue 28 with cover illustrated by Milton Glaser.
Editors: Tiffany Lee Brown, Jon Raymond, Joshua Berger; Art
director: Berger.

{ JOSHUA BERGER

PLAZM

*J*oshua Berger is a cofounder and creative director of Plazm, a design firm that publishes innovative art, design, cultural, and literary works worldwide. The studio builds brand identities, advertising, custom typography, and interactive and retail experiences.

Why did you launch Plazm?

Plazm was formed by a group of artists who were dissatisfied with the avenues of expression available to them. We were talking about things like media control and how we'd like to see artists representing artists. These discussions led to the launch of *Plazm* magazine.

Plazm is a type foundry, magazine, and book publisher, and other entrepreneurial ventures. Is it part of your design collective or separate?

Plazm has grown organically, garden-like. Some shoots sprout up and take hold for a long time, others only last a few seasons. The type foundry grew out of the experimental design that our magazine came to be known for in the early 1990s. The books came from the same idea as the magazine—to produce content that interests us and is perhaps marginalized by mainstream media. The design firm arose naturally from the mass of creative energy at the magazine and our need to support our magazine habit. Client work is really what ends up paying the bills.

What are the most important concerns for Plazm? Art or commerce?

Plazm magazine has never made any money. In the beginning, we all had other jobs and worked on the magazine on the side. Starting in 1993, we tried to subsidize it with Plazm Fonts, which helped, but never really brought in enough to put us in the black. In 1995,

we decided to take the form/content/ideas we had been exploring in *Plazm* magazine and apply them to commercial design work. This is what has sustained us. The irony now is that the magazine is still something we do on the side and Plazm Design has become the day job.

So you are servers as well as creators?

Sometimes dichotomies arise. For instance, there will never be an instance of censorship in the magazine or on our website. However, this uncompromising position has cost us more than a few advertisers over the years. As a commercial design studio that is helping multinational corporations market their products, is it worthwhile if their payments enable us to distribute political and cultural materials via our magazine, books and antiwar posters? I often wonder. Of course, designers partnering with corporations can also do good work. Our baseline is to maintain a 50/50 split between clients and causes.

Has the type business subsidized the other activities, or have you managed to be self-sufficient?

Neither *Plazm* magazine nor Plazm Fonts could have been self-sufficient without Plazm Design to support them. However, all of the things cross-pollinate in positive ways. The typographic expertise developed through Plazm Fonts has allowed us to do custom alphabets for corporate clients. We have designed typefaces for MTV, Nike, and Starbucks. This knowledge has directly informed the creation of custom letterforms for brand identity work.

(Above) "Box of Rocks" article from *Plazm*. Art direction: Joshua Berger; illustration and design: Drew Marshall.

Of course, designers partnering with corporations can also do good work. Our baseline is to maintain a 50/50 split between clients and causes.

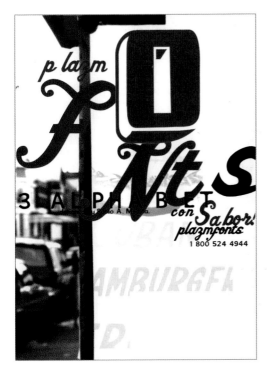

Advertisement for Plazm's custom Fonts: Cuba, Vitrina, North Bergen. Font and ad designer: Pablo Medina; client: Plazm Fonts

The magazine may not make money, but it serves a purpose?
A noncommercial, highly creative experience like the magazine has taught us, in a different way than a commercial job, how to help designers, illustrators, writers, photographers, and artists find and channel their passion. The result is often great and interesting work. We take this experience in collaboration and apply it to the paying work. Our clients, whether they know it or not, benefit tremendously from what we've all learned publishing *Plazm* magazine.

Magazines are not easy to sustain. How has *Plazm* done so?
Advertising, trades, and paper company sponsorships fund the hard costs of magazine production. Design and editing costs are subsidized by Plazm's commercial client work. Newsstand and online sales account for some revenue as well. None of it would be possible without the unwavering support we get from contributors. Even after all these years, I'm excited and a little surprised when someone like Milton Glaser or Matthew Stadler agrees to design a cover or write an intensive interview, without pay. It's like we're tending this massive bonfire. Creative people want to come warm themselves, but they also want to throw logs on the coals. Fires aren't always easy to sustain, but would you want life without them? Sustaining the magazine works the same way. Time and sacrifice are just part of the deal.

How important is design to your entire endeavor?
Design is absolutely critical. It is through design that messages reach people most effectively. Designers are trained in methods of mass communication and propaganda; we have a vast potential as agents for social change. I believe design can change the world.

{ PETER BILAK

TYPOTHEQUE

Peter Bilak is a graphic designer who works in editorial, graphic, type, and Web design. His studio in The Hague, Netherlands, specializes in the creation of custom fonts. He is cofounder of dot dot dot magazine and is a contributing editor of Deleatue magazine based in Prague.

Why did you start Typotheque?

I started the website in 1999 with an idea to publish some fonts. I chose the name because I liked the connection with "bibliotheque" and thought we could possibly publish books (we did publish our first book in 2004). It was only in 2001 that the site also started working commercially and turned into a distribution channel for all related projects: *dot dot dot* magazine, books I made, diaries, T-shirts, fonts, and so on. In 2006, my wife Johanna joined me as partner and we both started spending most of our time with Typotheque.

How did Arabic type come to be?

The Arabic project was initiated by the Khatt foundation for Arabic typography. They have noted that most of the publishing in the Middle East is bilingual, yet very few typefaces function side by side. Arabic usually appears inferior next to Latin because of the formal attributes of Arabic, which descends below the baseline and looks smaller. So I started researching Arabic type, which is not based on calligraphy, with an intention to create a civil, secular type, clearly distinct from the Islamic tradition of calligraphy, a formalization of fast handwriting that corresponds with my earlier typeface, Fedra. It was a very long process in which I learned a lot and it led to other non-Latin projects.

Is creating type a viable business? Indeed, what is your business model?

In general, creating typefaces is not very profitable. The hours are very long and there are thousands of typefaces on the market that sell for a few dollars on a CD, so the

(Left) Dutch Postage Stamps (right) and working sketches for Typotheque typefaces Design: Typotheque/Peter Bilak.

conclusion after speaking to a financially minded person would be that it doesn't make sense to spend time with type. Initially, it was a desire to create books, texts, and photos, as well as render them in typefaces that I design. I didn't count the hours because I had other paying projects and type is a labor of love. But after a few years it reversed, and the type started to pay off, and now it helps to finance future projects.

How much of your practice is devoted to your entrepreneurial pursuit versus client work?

The ratio changes every year and now I think only about 20 percent of the projects are client driven. We could probably make do without them, but I really enjoy client projects, so we'll keep them. They are usually exhibitions that we author, curate and design: books, printed matter, and videos.

What is your biggest success and why?

I suppose the biggest success is that our activities have continued for many years now and it seems that they will continue. I remember the day I quit a job. I woke up the next day with the thought that I am on my own now. I still find it amazing that after one project is finished something else comes up, without a business plan or model, and we manage to support ourselves.

the font: Cantara-Bold
r: /tehmarbuta.fina/yeh.medi/beh.init/reh.fina/kaf.medi/lam.init/alef.isol/space/tah.isol/
khah.medi/lam.init/alef.isol
Tue Jul 25 13:49:30 20
Page

{ CONSTANTIN BOYM

SOUVENIRS AT THE END OF THE CENTURY

*C*onstantin Boym was born in Moscow, studied design in Italy, and in 1986, founded Boym Partners Inc. in New York. His studio produces tableware for Alessi, watches for Swatch, exhibit installations, home products, and gifts including "missing monuments," miniature replicas of famous buildings, and lenticular clocks. Objects produced at his studio are in the permanent collection of the Museum of Modern Art.

You've been creating your disaster souvenirs, called Buildings of Disaster, for a number of years. They include monuments, like the World Trade Center. What prompted you to make them?

It started in 1997 as a three-year-long project. Recognizing that the end of a century generates a particular mood of introspection, a desire to look back and to reminiscence, we decided to create limited editions of unusual souvenirs based on the century's troubled history. The most controversial, and the most successful, among the souvenirs was a collection called "Buildings of Disaster," the monuments of tragic or terrible events. Some of these buildings may have been prized architectural landmarks, others nondescript anonymous structures. But disaster changes everything. The images of burning or exploded buildings make a different, populist history of architecture, one based on emotional involvement rather than on scholarly appreciation.

Where did the ideas come from?

The information for making the miniatures came from the pages of newspapers and magazines. From the beginning, I made the decision not to get too archival, but rather operate with what had already been sifted through media representations. It felt important not to get into architectural details, but to allow for generalizations and even distortions to heighten the emotional impact of the objects. Made of bonded nickel, the miniature buildings have a substantial weight and a feel of solid metal.

There seems to be an endless number of these. Which are the most popular sellers?

Twenty-one have been made to date. Six buildings were produced for the original catalog in 1997, including the miniature of the Twin Towers as the site of the deadly bombing of 1993. All production was supposed to stop after the century's official end on December 31, 2000. Nine months later, the weeks that followed the tragic day of September 11, 2001 changed our plans. To my amazement, we got inundated with requests for the souvenirs, specifically for that sold-out miniature of the 1993 World Trade Center. Orders came even from former occupants of the Twin Towers who survived the deadly attack of September 11. After much hesitation and soul-searching, we made a decision to reissue the World Trade Center miniature as a fundraising effort, donating the proceeds to charity. Later that year, we produced the September 11 Memorial Set, which included a new miniature of the Center and one of the Pentagon. Eventually, the editions of Buildings of Disaster continued with more new monuments, the edition of each limited to 500 pieces.

Did you create them to actually make money or art? Or can both be done at the same time?

I am surprised at this question. Art, of course! To make matters more complicated, I do not think of "Buildings of Disaster" as art, either. For me, they are objects of design, not art. Their distribution channel is a store, or mail-order catalog, and their price ($110 apiece), while not exactly cheap, is certainly not a typical art price. Of course, the function of the souvenir objects is "fuzzy"; they fulfill an immaterial need. You can't brush your teeth with them, as one of my design teachers used to say. People put their own meaning into the miniatures and they find their own personal ways to use them as material for memories.

How do you sell these products?
Due to the sensitive nature of these objects, we had to handle the commercial part with care. We usually ask for a store to display the objects separately and in a dignified way, accompanied with a small text that explains our design intent. Only a handful of special, high-end stores have the interest and desire to do this. We also sell them on our own website, of course, where everything is well presented and displayed.

How do you deal with the criticism that, despite their overt irony, perhaps a few are in bad taste?
Journalists like to question me about negative responses when, in reality, there were just a handful of complaints over all these years. Few people objected on the grounds of taste; some were unhappy about commercialization of disaster. In truth, if people were truly unhappy with this project, it would have stopped years ago.

Buildings of Disaster: The Empire State Building (when the World War II bomber hit the building) is one in a series of satiric souvenirs. Design: Boym Partners Inc.

Buildings of Disaster:
Miniature Twin Towers
designed to commemorate
the tragedy of September 11.

Buildings of Disaster: Ford's Theater, commemorating
the site of Abraham Lincoln's assassination by John
Wilkes Booth.

Buildings of Disaster: Unabomber Shack, commemorating the
hideaway of the Kozinsky the infamous Unabomber. Design:
Boym Partners Inc.

Buildings of Disaster: Neverland commemorating Michael Jackson's pleasure palace and estate.

(Left) Buildings of Disaster: Federal Building, commemorating the terrorist attack on the Alfred P. Murrah Federal Building in Okalahoma City, Okalahoma. (Right) New Orleans Superdome, after Hurricane Katrina ravaged the city. Design: Boym Partners Inc.

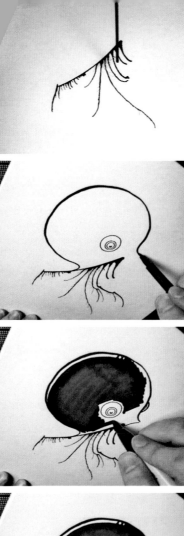

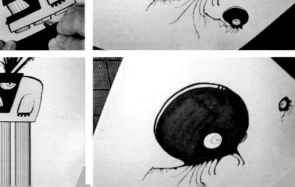

WHAT'S THE STORY?

POST YOURS AT DAILYMONSTER.COM

{ STEFAN G. BUCHER

THE DAILY MONSTER

*S*tefan G. Bucher leads the graphic design firm, 344, in Los Angeles. He specializes in CD cover design and his clients include Arista, Atlantic, Capitol, Dreamworks, Interscope, Maverick, Transport, TVT, and Warner Bros. Records. For a year, he has been host to "Daily Monster: A Growing Collection of Curious Creatures and the Stories Behind Them," a blog feature whereby he introduces a clan of monstrous creations into the virtual world.

What prompted you to start the Daily Monster?
One afternoon in the spring of 2006, I was driving across town and just as I was entering downtown L.A., I got an image in my mind of an inky monster wound around my arm. I should say right up front that I don't drink or take drugs. Images like that just pop into my head. I went home and started making monsters.

I gathered the first 50 creatures in a book called *Upstairs Neighbors* and tried finding a publisher to put it out. But the publishers I talked to either said no or took forever to make up their minds. I started the blog and the Daily Monsters to take my mind off the waiting and to have something to send to the various editors as a little reminder. As it turned out, of course, the "promo clips" became a much bigger deal than the original book proposal and opened up all kinds of new possibilities.

Would you call the Daily Monster a blog? Or is it more an art/design project?
The Daily Monster is definitely more of an art project than a blog. Mind you, it began as part of my then two-month-old blog, which was then called 344 LOVES YOU, and was a sort of production diary of my day-to-day work. As soon as the monsters came along, though, the non-design audience grew so quickly that the new focus was clear. They wanted fresh creatures, not my reports about last night's problem with the printer.

(Left) The Daily Monster strip and (above) DailyMonster. com homepage and video. Illustration/design: Stefan G. Bucher.

To get the word out, particularly in a saturated blogosphere, you must promote DM and yourself. How do you go about doing this?

I have always relied on the kindness of strangers. A few days into the first 100 Daily Monsters, I sent a link to Bryony Gomez-Palacio at SpeakUp and to Ze Frank. Both were nice enough to write a few kind words and link their sites to mine. My visitor stats quadrupled in two days and quadrupled again within the following two weeks. Since then, I've been lucky enough to have some loyal readers and contributors that follow the site and put out the word when new things are happening.

Internet sites do not cost a lot of capital, only time and talent. How are you funding your project?

Luckily, talent is a renewable resource. The more I work, the more I can work.

The main investment is time, of which I don't have nearly enough. Initially, the cost was that the monsters were taking up all my billable hours and I barely had time to take care of my commercial clients. Taking on new clients was out of the question at that point. But within a matter of a few months, the monsters have brought me a number of great new jobs.

How important is YouTube to your propagation of the Monster faith?

The monster faith! I like that! Does that make me the Ink Pope? Pope Sumi the First? Everything started with YouTube. That's where I initially hosted all the monsters and it allowed them to spread very quickly. Right now, my primary host for the videos is Revver, which pays me a small royalty for every completed view, but I still put all the clips on YouTube as well. It seems to be a totally separate

ecosystem from my regular site. There isn't a lot of crossover at all. No matter how many times I extend the invitation at the end of the clips, people who see the monsters on YouTube usually won't come to dailymonster.com. It just seems to be the way that is.

How much of DM is strategic and how much is pure intuitive delight?
There is a little bit of strategy in getting the word out, but it's all in the service of the intuitive delight. I've never done drawings that have been as fun as the monsters. A lot of my other stuff is incredibly intricate and labor intensive. I love that work, too, but only after it's done. The monsters I love while I'm doing them. They make my brain feel good. They make me laugh

(Left) Store344.com web pages, produced by FWIS, and (right) 344design.com web page by Daniel D. Holmes each is an outreach to new readers and consumers of The Daily Monster and other products. Illustration/design: Stefan G. Bucher.

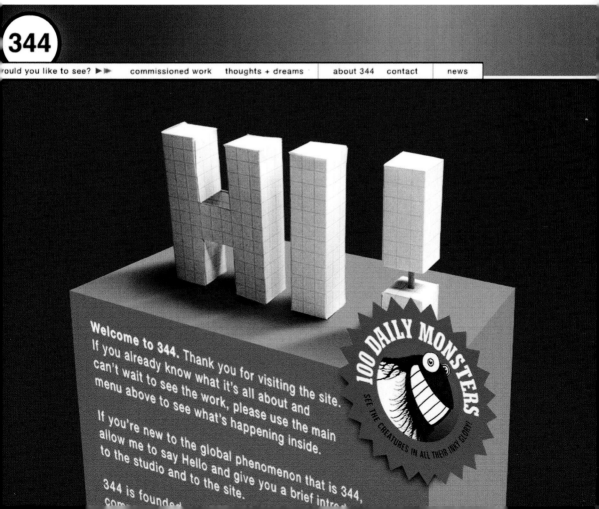

{ DEBORAH BUCK

BUCK HOUSE

*D*eborah Buck, proprietor of Buck House in New York, is an artist and designer. She has a proclivity for finding the unusual during her extensive travels throughout the world, in search of the finest art objects and furniture for her antiques shop on Madison Avenue. She also runs a gallery nearby where she curates exhibitions that mix art, furniture, and objects.

You started as a painter and a good one at that. Why did you decide to start an antique store?

After having my son, Sam, I found the isolation of the studio too confining and wanted to work collaboratively with other creative people. My first job was drawing and designing animated characters and I wanted to return to that kind of collective design work. The notion of a "design lab" has always been very attractive to me. The store began as a way to interact with other designers and to feed my passion for furniture, art, and objects.

You are not trained as a designer, but you are a design mediator in terms of the interiors you produce and the consulting you do for clients. What about design appeals to you most?

About 10 years ago, I realized that my interest in interiors and decorative arts was becoming another passion of mine and a source of great creative pleasure. Since I operate from a painter's head, the entirety of design exists along the same plane for me. The arranging of furniture is the same as the arranging of color and form on a canvas; it's just 3-D. I love paintings, but I love the process of painting more. The process of designing is where one grows and learns. Design is a passion and I'm interested in any art form that requires a passion to produce excellence.

Buck House is your store and you have created a brand around it in which you are the brand character, so to speak. What's so important about making this brand?

Early on at Buck House, I discovered that the items that I brought from my own home sold more quickly, regardless of price, than items that I bought for the shop. It was at that point that I began to own my vision and I began only to buy items that I would want in my own home. I am fairly fearless when it comes to interiors and that's what fuels the energy. My clients look to me to validate their choices. Branding is a contemporary "Good Housekeeping Seal of Approval," only much more sophisticated in my case. It makes insecure customers who are unsure of their own taste feel more comfortable letting me make their choices for them. The branding of Buck House is the frame for the painting. It has allowed me to create my own little realm where I make and break the rules. It is a cheerleading squad for Buck House.

Over the past few years, you've expanded your role. What does the Buck brand now include? Some you create, others you commission.

The Buck House brand now encompasses the original boutique of Buck House, The Gallery at Buck House, and the Buck House Estate Jewelry Collection. The website, www.buckhouse.biz, which also features my blog "Buckstops," is another world of its own, bringing Buck House to doors as far away as Dubai.

Valentine card from Buck House paying homage to glamour patron saint, Elizabeth Taylor; photo: Stan Wan.

You curate exhibitions on particular themes. What is your strategy with this? Is it to generate more consumer interest or to explore your own interests in art and design?

The exhibits are to satiate my interests, but also to publicize where I'm going, what I'm doing, and what my latest interest is. "Manhattan Glamour" was the opening show and its purpose was to launch the gallery at Buck House as a glamorous place where a scene could be found. I'm very attracted to glamour and I think that it is what sets Buck House apart from many other antique businesses. The Buck House look is that of informed glamour, glamour with content. The "Blue" show was a way to continue the branding of "Buck House Blue," to firmly establish my connection to my color and to publicize my theories about color in general. The "Gem" show was to celebrate and announce the opening of the Buck House Estate Jewelry Collection to the world. The most recent exhibit, "Wild Flowers," takes what could be considered a tame and easy topic and presents the subject through difficult, abstract, and sophisticated contemporary work.

(Top) Interior of Buck House on Madison Avenue featuring its trademark turquoise and magenta stripes. Photo: Douglas Friedman

(Bottom) Promo card "The conversation continues between art, antiques and objects." Photo: Wan.

(Far right) A tableau in Buck House Blue surrounding Deborah Buck's Thermonuclear Blue Flower, acrylic on paper with glitter, 2006. Photo: Wan.

Various Kidrobot characters in the Gorillaz 2-Tone series designed by Jamie Hewlett

{ PAUL BUDNITZ

KIDROBOT

P aul Budnitz is the founder of Kidrobot in New York that produces limited-edition toys and apparel, fusing graphic design, fine art, illustration, industrial design, graffiti, and music. Over the past five years, he has launched a Kidrobot store and gallery in New York, Los Angeles, and San Francisco.

Why did you found Kidrobot?

At the time, I was working on an animated film and I became addicted to a lot of the limited-edition toys I saw coming out of Japan and Hong Kong. I eventually flew to China and convinced some factories to help me make toys of my own.

Have you always been a comics and/or toy fanatic beforehand?

I was totally into comics for quite a long time. But I'm influenced by all kinds of things, especially fashion design. I love Louis Vuitton and Marc Jacobs and all the packaging that makes things precious. I like Japanese designers such as Comme des Garcons and Hysteric Glamor. And I like fashion trends in general. I just love mods, goths, and death rockers—all that early 1980s subculture stuff I grew up with. You can see that influence in some of our designs. I avoid kitsch, retro, or campy art. We have a big sign on the wall of our office that reads, "Nostalgia is Death."

The aesthetic of Kidrobot toys is so decidedly different than even the best character-based toys that migrated into comic book stores. What made you think this could be a viable business?

Kidrobot has a very specific design aesthetic. When I began the stores, and began designing and making our own toys, the stuff we were making was just so exciting, so bright, and plastic, and colorful, and I just love it all. Why wouldn't people buy it? It's so amazing! I realize that isn't very scientific, but I can't see another way to judge original creative work. If you get too analytical about it, you're not producing art.

At the same time, on the business side, this company has always been incredibly well thought-out. I have a background in computer programming (among the random things I've done, I programmed software for nuclear power plants when I was just out of high school). So there's a custom computer back end that I built when I realized I couldn't buy software that would do what I wanted it to do. We rely heavily on computers for stocking and sales analysis as a way to keep our staff and stock levels lean.

Meat & Cheese Three-inch Dunny by Travis Cain at Planet Propaganda. Dunny is the open-ended signature character for Kidrobot.

You get the right people in a room, create enough heat and pressure, and don't allow much time, and something amazing emerges all on its own.

What is the business model? It's obviously not about volume.

If I make just 200 pieces of a toy or a piece of clothing, then I only need to find 200 people willing to buy it. In a way, it's not so different than what other luxury manufacturers are doing. If Gucci makes a limited-edition handbag, that handbag costs much more than the standard model. The challenge is, of course, that sometimes we make something beautiful and it's limited edition, so we can't make more of them even if we want to make more money. That's only a problem if you don't have any other ideas for things to make, but I really live in abundance of creativity, and faith in that abundance, and I really don't find this a problem.

You hit on a great idea with Munny and Dunny, where the user could customize the products. How did this idea develop?

A Japanese company had been doing something similar. We sort of adopted and expanded the idea for the United States and Tristan Eaton and I created Dunny as a really great palate for artists—there is a big round face and a really beautiful, smooth body design. Munny evolved out of the fact that all these people were buying painted Dunnys from us, then repainting them, and selling them on eBay. It was (still is) a big scene—some of the custom toys go for a few thousand dollars. So Munny is a do-it-yourself toy. The toy is beautiful on its own, unpainted. We have a

Custom designed members of the French Dunny Series by Various Artists.

giant six-foot version that is covered with chalkboard paint and is currently living in the Cooper-Hewitt (Smithsonian) Design Triennial.

Do the designers and artists who contribute their ideas come to you or you to them?
Mostly people come to us or they are friends of friends. Kidrobot is all about relationship and community. There are so many opportunities coming at us that we don't spend too much time going out looking for new ones. We're still trying to catch up!

What about in-house design?
A lot of the stuff is done in-house. Characters like Moochy and Pooty, Munny, Dunny and Zoomies and our entire clothing line were developed in house, either by myself or in collaboration with really amazing illustrators.

What in the creative process do you value the most?
There is a moment when you are generating new ideas, especially in a group, and something magical just pops out. I love that. Group creativity is really an alchemical process, and it's one thing I seem to have a talent for. You get the right people in a room, create enough heat and pressure, and don't allow much time, and something amazing emerges all on its own. Something is invoked.

(Top) Eight-inch Obey Dunny by Shepard Fairey. (Middle) Kidrobot Robot Head Hoodie. (Bottom) Ace & Ion by Tara McPherson.

{ NICHOLAS CALLAWAY

CALLAWAY ARTS & ENTERTAINMENT

icholas Callaway is the founder and CEO of Callaway Arts & Entertainment in New York City. His firm specializes in family entertainment across all media: book publishing, animation, film, television, and product design. For many years, Callaway packaged books by the pop star Madonna, art photographer David La Chappelle, and other creative luminaries. His collaboration with toy maker and illustrator David Kirk has grown into a line of products, animated TV programs, and fashions.

How important is design to your company?
I'm not interested in making, using, or buying anything that isn't well designed and well made, purposefully and whole heartedly.

You were not trained as a designer, but you are a veteran publishing maven. Did you have to develop the "taste" for good design or was that a given?
I believe that you either have an eye or you don't. Studying photography from the age of 14 trained and developed my eye, but I must have been born with it.

One of your most "famous/infamous" books was Madonna's *Sex*. that was designed by Fabien Baron. Did you act as art director? And by extension, how do you art direct your projects?
Fabien is a great art director and designer, and the book was an expression of his design sense, along with the photographer Steven Meisel. And Madonna is the meta creative director. She has as good an eye as any artist I've ever worked with. Our job was to translate their collective vision into a sensual use of materials—the Mylar wrap, stamped aluminum covers, the uncoated paper, the comic book, and so on. The mandate was to translate the sensibility of the limited-edition *livre d'artiste* into a book aimed at a mass audience (for instance, few people realize that each copy is numbered, stamped into the back cover). Madonna said she wanted a book that was unlike any other book ever published, completely new and different.

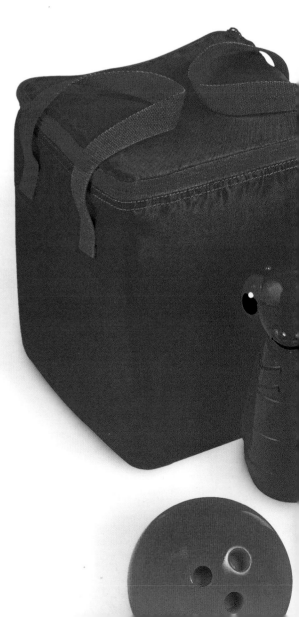

Your books are only one component of an overall entertainment company that involves products and television. How has the marketplace changed since you began as a book packager?

We're focused primarily on family entertainment these days, creating children's characters and stories that can have life across books, television, consumer products, and the Web. We're in the midst of building Sunnypatch.com as a Web destination for young children and their parents. This reflects the fact that we live in a multi platform era with the Web as the primary medium for the next generation of kids.

How have you changed your strategies since beginning your company?

When I began, I wanted to create very expensive products for a small audience. Now we create inexpensive products for a global audience.

To accomplish this, you obviously integrate these various media. What goes into your decision making? Do you test? Or do you intuit?

It takes a long time to build a brand, and it's very difficult; therefore, we only undertake projects that we believe have real potential to exist in many media and that are worth the years of time, energy, and investment.

The Sunny Patch Kids products were designed by David Kirk and creatively directed by Callaway Entertainment. The colorful toys, clothes, and this playhouse derive from Kirk's children's book illustrations, which serve as the launch pad for this entrepreneurial line.

Bowl-O-Rama, designed by Kirk, is a fun way for kids to bowl by knocking down the little lizards.

Kirk transforms the fanciful insect creations in *Miss Spider's Tea* Party into fun, outdoor stuff for kids including the Ladybug Tent, thermos, pail, boots, and owl watering ca

What has been your most challenging project as an entrepreneur and why?

The most challenging project has been to take something that was conceived as a single book, *Miss Spider's Tea Party*, and build it into a cross-platform lifestyle brand, Sunny Patch, that encompasses a book series of 40 titles with six million copies sold, a computer-animated television series that is broadcast in more than fifty countries, a lifestyle brand of 600 products with twelve million units sold in 1,500 Target Stores nationwide, and soon, Sunnypatch.com, an online world aimed at children and their parents.

How do you decide which ideas to put your limited resources behind?

It must take my breath away creatively and make my marketing mind race. Then the entire team tries to poke holes in it. I sleep on it, and if I still feel the same way a week later, then we're good to go.

If you were to state a business philosophy, or even just a motto, what would it be?

"There, that wasn't so easy, was it?"

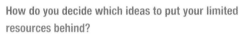

Written and designed by Kirk, *Miss Spider's Tea Party* started as a simple children's book and grew into an animated series, products, and clothes.

For this golf set, Kirk draws on the characters from *Miss Spider's Tea Party.*

{ TINA CHANG & ESTHER MUN

START HERE NOTEBOOKS

Esther Mun studied design at The School of Visual Arts in New York. She first practiced design at Pentagram before becoming a key member of the Duffy & Partners design team. Tina Chang also studied design at The School of Visual Arts before beginning her graphic design career at Pentagram. She then worked as a senior designer at MTV, a consultant to The Public Theater, and a senior art director at Martha Stewart Living Omnimedia. She and Mun founded Start Here and Little Fury Design Studio, NY, in 2006.

What inspired you to become Start Here?

EM: We were each independently aspiring to achieve more than the next hot job to pad our resume or continuing to climb the corporate ladder of someone else's design firm. We both wanted to make something of our own that reflected our common design principles, aesthetics, beliefs, and interests. Start Here is our design playground—a place where we can design the way we want to design and make products that we had previously only daydreamed about. The Start Here notebooks are the first in a line of many manifestations of this shared vision. They reinforce our belief in the importance of the everyday person's interaction with, and contribution to, design. The modular system encourages users to customize their book to reflect their own taste and needs. Our name and tagline, "Start Here: Where will you take it?" reflects this idea that our products are only providing a starting point.

These notebooks are based on a unique modular system. How did this come about?

TC: Early on in our brainstorming sessions, we decided that our first project as Start Here would focus on re-thinking the notebook. We challenged ourselves to make a truly unique product that reflected our design principles: functionality, simplicity, and individuality. Esther's method of stitching one sketchbook to another until four books were attached to form one notebook was a source of inspiration. We really loved this all-in-one concept where

the user decides which books they'd like together, and we started to ask ourselves, "How can we link this together in the most intuitive, functional way?" After lots of explorations and drafts, some of which were pretty ridiculous, we devised our present linking system that provided a singular, inter-changeable source for all your notes, maps, calendar, addresses, and more.

How much of your design practice is devoted to producing your Start Here line?

EM: We devote as much time as possible to the Start Here line, but since we are running two businesses simultaneously, we aim for a 50/50 balance between Start Here and Little Fury (our design service entity). When we can spend more time on Start Here, we're thrilled.

What learning curves did you have to follow to get this far along in your business?

TC: Our biggest challenges always involve money and efficiency. How do we develop new products, promote and maintain our current stock, work as a design agency, and still pay the rent and ourselves? It's a delicate balance, and we are still in the process of learning this part of the business. We connect with other small business owners to learn from their experiences and try to head off those inevitable small business pitfalls when we can. But complications still come up, and it is from these that we learn the most.

The Start Here line of modular, efficient, customizable notebooks for work and home. Design: Esther Mun and Tina Chang.

Which of you does what? Do you separate functions between business and commerce?

TC: At Start Here and Little Fury, we divide and conquer in a surprisingly natural way. We're both designers, so no one person is in charge of either all business matters or all visual ideas. We're truly a team and collectively manage design projects and develop products. Our strengths and weaknesses lie in complementary areas, so we tend to know who would be best suited to a certain job. It's very strange, but perfect at the same time.

What have you done to protect your product?

EM: We registered a provisional patent for the linking system and are in the process of getting a utility patent. With so much on our plate, having a lawyer to explain each step and file all the paperwork has been indispensable to us.

Financially, how do you support your business?

EM: We support Start Here with the income from our client-based design studio, Little Fury. We welcome clients who pay well and on time. We have also taken a personal pay cut to support Start Here, but as it is something we believe in, it continues to be worth it.

How successful have you been? Have you found your audience?

TC: Since our launch in March 2007, we have been continually working to promote the Start Here brand. Online sales through our website (starthereny.com) have been great. Bloggers are the new word-of-mouth and

we've seen substantial growth as Start Here has been included in several blogs and daily emails. We've been fortunate to be featured in several magazines with more on the horizon. We have found that diversifying our press exposure is key to reaching as many users as possible. We also get a lot of feedback. We read every email to really understand and develop a good relationship with our audience. Due to the nonexclusive nature of our products (a direct result of our design principles), our audience is really quite broad.

{ SEYMOUR CHWAST
THE NOSE

S*eymour Chwast, who cofounded Push Pin Studios in 1957, is an artist, illustrator, and designer. He has authored over 30 children's books, as well as an equal number of adult books. He edited, published, and art directed* Push Pin Graphic, *cofounded* Push Pin Press, *and is currently the designer and publisher of* The Nose, *which is published quarterly.*

What inspired you to start *The Nose*?
Originally, James Victore and Steve Brower were going to produce *The Nose* with me. Steven created the second issue on Huey Long but James didn't do any issues, so I carried on. *The Nose*, along with other studio publications I've been involved with, was prompted by our interest in promoting ourselves. It also exposed the kind of work we wanted to do.

You've engaged in many entrepreneurial ventures. Did you always do these as respites from the daily commercial activities of your studio or to actually turn a profit?
I could never hope to make a profit with *The Nose*, but the possibilities were there with other projects. It was a way to create products that we could own and could be another outlet for our talent.

How do you distribute the publication?
It is sent to designers, art directors, editors, our clients, friends, and colleagues.

It seems that you are always going hat in hand to the paper companies and printers to get *The Nose* produced? Has this been a difficult process for you?
Our printers and paper mills want to reach the same people we want to reach. We create ads for them in each issue. The issues themselves demonstrate the quality of printing and paper, which are provided at little or no cost. It is quid pro quo and therefore not a tough sell.

Each issue has a different theme—some are social/political, others are more carefree (like "Hair"). What determines a theme?
The themes try not to advance any particular agenda. However, the serious ones may, not so seriously, express our liberal bent. The others are culled from popular culture. The nature of the publication and its limited space, however, do not allow us to explore any theme with depth. We try to make the most of humor and satire.

What are the most successful *Noses* and why?
I like the ones on ethnic epithets, magic, and war. I can't tell you which ones were most successful because we never surveyed readers.

And while we're at it, why do you call this *The Nose*?
Eye, the respected design magazine, inspired me. A nose is funnier than an eye and therefore sets the right tone.

Aside from your irrepressible desire to make art and design, what do you think *The Nose* has contributed to its audience?
The Nose's predecessors, the *Push Pin Almanack* and *Push Pin Graphic*, helped to make a reputation for the studio. I encourage young designers and illustrators to follow our example.

What's next for your entrepreneurial side?
I would like to continue designing typefaces, and designing, and illustrating all kinds of books.

(Top eft) The first issue of *The Nose*, published in 2000, was designed as a promotion to show off Seymour Chwast's work, but turned into a commentary on the state of the world.

(Top right) Magic tricks, and dirty tricks, and everything in between came under scrutiny in this issue from 2005.

(Bottom) This issue, from 2006, was devoted to all the scandals that come out in the wash, from famous political scandals to steamy love affairs.

⊠ WHO BROUGHT THE RUM?

Props from a client film we shot that is so secret we will probably never, ever be able to tell you about it except to say that it involved us buying up pretty much all the Tiki cocktail umbrellas in the Chicagoland area.

⊠ OVER THE AIR ALL OVER THE PLACE

Hot Air Rises

Here's the audio from Jim and Brendan Dawes' Making Your Short Attention Span Pay Big Dividends presentation from SXSW 2006. Edward Lifson invited Jim over to the WBEZ studios for Sunday's Chicago Public Radio arts show *Hello Beautiful!* You can listen to it, or download it, here.

Also, here's Jim with type projected all over his face, giving a rambling presentation for the Society of Graphic Designers of Canada and here's the audio of the Opening Remarks at last year's SXSW Interactive Conference in Austin, from Jim and Jason Fried of 37signals.

TAKE AWAY THINGS UNTIL YOU'RE DONE

What We Talk About When We Talk About Work

When we first started out, we were known for long headlines with pointed punch lines. No one remembers why, although a few of them can still make us chuckle.

These days we're all about stripping away. Fewer words in our copy, fewer lines in our designs. No one remembers when that happened, either. More...

ABOUT COUDAL PARTNERS

As of Late

Our name, logo and indentity for a new upscale pizza/wine concept, La Madia. Our friend Dan Pink asked us to create this visual metaphor and a site for his whip-smart new book *A Whole New Mind.* So we did. We also created a site for *Cast of Shadows,* the first novel from CP alum Kevin Guilfoile. We've recently formed a new company with Jake Walker, Eric Welsh and Richard Jones. It's called The Show and it's off to a booming start with partnerships with The Pixies and Dead Can Dance. We're also working on a couple super-secret branding projects, promoting a fight for The United Center and Don King Productions, creating and implementing the Go Roma brand, designing materials including this animation, for First Look, and creating just about everything for a new golf concept called The Groove. We're also working on projects for an NHL team, a bank, a venture capital firm, a regional sports network, a media company and a farm. Phew.

Plus we're having a gas building our Jewelboxing and Lowercase Tee brands and plotting to take over the web.

RECENT PRESS

PC Mag just named us as one of their Top 99 Undiscovered Websites. JC took part in a Communication Arts Magazine roundtable on design and technology and was interviewed by Samantha Stainburn for Crain's Chicago Business recently. Another interview is Under the Iron and another roundtable happened as a part of 37signals' Fireside Chat series. JC wrote a piece for A List Apart. Time Magazine named our Museum of Online Museums (MoOM) one of their 50 Coolest Websites for 2005. There was a big CP profile in UK magazine, Computer Arts. Bob Mehr got into The Show for The Chicago Reader. Wired wrote about our Dear Cell-Phone User Cards. Plus, Time Out Magazine and The Christian Science Monitor both reviewed our Field-Tested Books project.

TWENTY MARKS

Here's a small sampling of logomarks we have created for a variety of clients. Use the plus signs below to navigate.

```
+ + + + + + + + +
+ + + + + + + + +
```

THIS STUDIO

At any given time we're working on a limited number of projects, but we do a lot of different things. Television, print, identity, interactive, brand development and a lot of outside stuff to keep things interesting.

400 North May Street
Chicago Illinois
USA 60622
312 243 1107

A THING WE MADE: JEWELBOXING

We hated the options available for custom packaging DVDs and CDs so we created a brand that gives creative professionals and hobbyists the tools to make great stuff. Here's a bit from the latest Jewelboxing weblog entry:

"Since using Jewelboxing, we have seen the sales of our sets increase dramatically - in fact we have seen the two best months out of 2 years already this year, because of these special collections." Read the entire post.

SOME OTHER THINGS WE MADE:

Pinsetter: Spell with buttons.

Limited-edition, professionally mixed and mastered, custom-designed live performances on CD. That's The Show. With partners like The Pixies and Dead Can Dance. More news soon.

Lowercase Tee: For politically and otherwise active kids.

{ JIM COUDAL
COUDALPARTNERS.COM

J im Coudal is founder and president of Coudal Partners, a design, advertising, and interactive studio in Chicago that develops online businesses including Jewelboxing, The Deck, and The Show.

When did you form Coudal Partners and why?
We're a design firm, sort of. Half of our work is brand, identity creation, and traditional design, and the other half is running Jewelboxing, The Deck, and The Show. I'm not exactly sure what we are. A small group of writers and artists is the best description. We have been in business for twelve years, but it's only in the last three or four that we have managed to move beyond being a traditional design consultancy and do work we really love pretty much every day.

You appear to be a virtual Web-generation machine. How and why did you decide to do so much on the Web, with sites, blogs, and so on?
Our site has been pretty popular since we launched it in 1999. At this point, I can't even conceive of us not being primarily independent Web publishers. One thing led to another and we were lucky enough to hit a really rough patch in 2002 that forced us to reevaluate what we were doing. So we tried to take greater control of our creative work and "free ourselves from the tyranny of clients," so to speak. There is a basic inequity in the work-for-hire model and we consciously have tried to break that habit in favor of creating products and services for an audience like ourselves.

How much of your firm's time and staff members are devoted to the Web business?
Probably 50 percent for the firm and 75 percent for me personally.

Pages from Coudal Partners website. The site is edited and designed by Coudal Partners as an ongoing experiment in web publishing, design and commerce.

How do you determine the content for your sites?
There's a famous theater review, I think it was by Edmund Wilson, that damned a play by saying, "People who like this sort of thing will find it exactly the kind of thing they like," but that's actually what we're about. People trust us to filter all sorts of things on the Web and those people must be like us in some essential way, otherwise why would they keep coming back? We have a wide variety of interests and we try to write and create things for ourselves mostly.

Have you made a profit through Web activity?
All of our Web-based businesses are profitable, and that allows us to be very picky about client projects we take on.

What does it mean, given your particular penchants, to be a design entrepreneur?
What we're trying to do is take control of the creative we produce in a meaningful and hopefully profitable way. The culture of the studio is based on the application of craft—typography, composition, filmmaking, writing, color theory, and so on—and also on learning, on getting smarter about design, technology, and commerce in service of creating things out of whole cloth. Typically, there's a company that wants to sell something, and there's an audience they want to sell it to; they hire us to mediate that, to facilitate

that communication. But it is infinitely more interesting and fulfilling if we can have all the seats at the table and eliminate the mediation. We want to be the seller and the audience. We want to target ourselves, so to speak. Building a large and loyal audience to our site was the first part, creating products that they and we need was secondary. Instead of, "If you build it, they will come," it's more, "If they come, you will build it."

So you prefer being your own client?
We do, in fact, love our clients, but we don't love all clients. We have relationships with generous and open-minded people who see a real advantage in our entrepreneurial stance because they get the benefit of what we learn, while we're making our own mistakes and performing all that application of craft as well. We even have client relationships in which we have traded our work for ownership in the brands or concepts we have developed. Having our own businesses gives us the flexibility to choose "work-for-hire" carefully.

That said, we do have this rule: We will do great work for a little money. We will do mediocre work for a ton of money. But we will not do mediocre work for a little money.

We have skills that marketers need and we do rent ourselves out to do it and part of that is to stay sharp and learn. The "getting up to speed" part of an assignment can be a lot of fun; learning a business quickly from the outside fast can spark all kinds of things or maybe come back later in one of our own concepts. We try to balance, but it seems we're always in the weeds with a little too much work to stay comfortable. I guess that chaos is addictive.

The movie webpage, which features a new clip daily. From the Coudal Partners website

TUESDAY EDITION

From a reader: "I could probably listen to the same song for five hours, but 'Dancing Queen?!?'" Steve's 238 Miles.

Field Tested Books webpage, a suitcase full of reviews of books read on location, edited by DR. From the Coudal Partners website

⚑ FIELD-TESTED BOOKS

It's a good time to catch up on our Field-Tested Books reading list. 47 personal reviews of books read in "a certain place" are online and free and if that's not enough, or you're a fan of portability and typography, or just have six extra bucks, we also have a book available as a PDF that includes 29 more, plus a sweet limited-edition, screened poster created by Aesthetic Apparatus. (Our reviews get reviewed in Time Out, The Christian Science Monitor and at Bookslut.)

{ DANIEL YOUNG

PARADOXY PRODUCTS

*D*aniel Young switched careers from being a lawyer to a designer/inventor and in 2005 founded Paradoxy Products. In its first two years, Paradoxy has marketed five completely new design objects that cross the borders between fun and philosophy and between design and art.

You were a lawyer. How and why did you enter the designed product business?

I was born with a designing mind and a lazy disposition. After college, law school was the easiest way to avoid real work. That led to a cushy career in law, which left me free to invent and design for myself, primarily to impress the accomplished woman who eventually became my wife.

(Top) Chess & Checkers set, product design by Daniel Young; graphic design by Marija Miljkovic; logo and technical support by Mirko Ilić. (Above) "Curb your God" T-shirt. Design: Young.

In my late forties, I felt the need to seek out my species and get feedback. Milton Glaser's work and his design thoughts convinced me he was one of the supreme designing minds of our time. So I sought him out and showed him my work, and he graciously consented to allow me to play in his studio part-time for the last 12 years of my legal career. Then I moved in full-time and played for three more years. Finally, my infantile desire to play matured into the slightly less infantile desire to have my work enter the real world and receive its proper recognition and recompense.

Mirko Ilić is working with you on the Swiss Army Card. It's such a sublimely simple idea. How was it conceived?

I guess the abstract idea of a multipurpose tool combined with the check-off format of vintage vacation postcards instantly crystallized as a card covering all the celebratory possibilities. The visual charm of the final product is due to the wonderful work of Mirko. Our designer, Marija, suggested that the universal happy face be converted to Swiss colors and Mirko topped it with a sly wink.

How did the "Curb Your God" T-shirt come to be?

The immediate stimuli were the events of September 11, 2001 and a call for related artwork from the Exit Gallery in New York. The original work on paper is now in the National Archive. But the problem of religious insanity had been on my mind for a long time, without reference to any particular religion. I thought it would be useful to use one of the popular methods of modern personal communication (the T-shirt) to send a message to all people whose religious beliefs might lead them to consider using violence. The vernacular of public signage seemed most appropriate, as did the conciseness of the phrase normally used to warn people to keep their dogs under control. It was the shortest message I could devise. It seems to have struck a chord.

How do you promote and sell these products?
I participate in trade shows such as the Museum Store Association Expo, the Toy Fair in Nuremberg, and the National Stationery Show with the objective of building a network of national and international sales representatives and finding appropriate customers. I communicate with stores whose design sense I admire. I send press releases to trade publications as well as publications that feature design products. I hope to achieve a certain critical mass, at which point information about my work begins to circulate in the media with the self-sustaining energy of a chain reaction.

Mozaniac is an idea that fits well in museum shops and boutiques. What is the genesis of this?
The unique puzzle pieces of Mozaniac grew out of the discovery of the bean-shaped yin-yang forms of the Mystery Magnets. The Mozaniac puzzle pieces are simply a "squaring" of the "bean." I made square beans and put slits in the center of all four sides.

That created a flat modular unit that could be combined with others endlessly by a sort of over/under weaving. The first "Eureka" moment came when I put four of them together and realized they had a physical integrity and made a nice puzzle if an image was placed on them and they were taken apart. The big "Eureka" came when I put six puzzle pieces together and put an image on the surface. I realized that under the surface, still completely blank, was enough material to make another picture. That meant I had discovered a simple puzzle system that could make two pictures on the same side (or four pictures if both sides were used).

Do you believe good design can move a product off the shelves?
Yes. Make that "great design" and it moves even further into the psyche of those who buy it. That is why I gave my company the slogan, "We Tickle The Psyche." In a nonthreatening way, I wanted to indicate that we have very deep objectives. Oné caveat: If the good or great design is also highly innovative, there must often be an educational process by which the consumer learns to appreciate it. This can slow the movement off the shelf.

Mozaniac Puzzle Systems, a simple puzzle system that allows the user to create two pictures on the same side, or four pictures if both sides are used. Product design: Daniel Young; graphic design: Miljkovic.

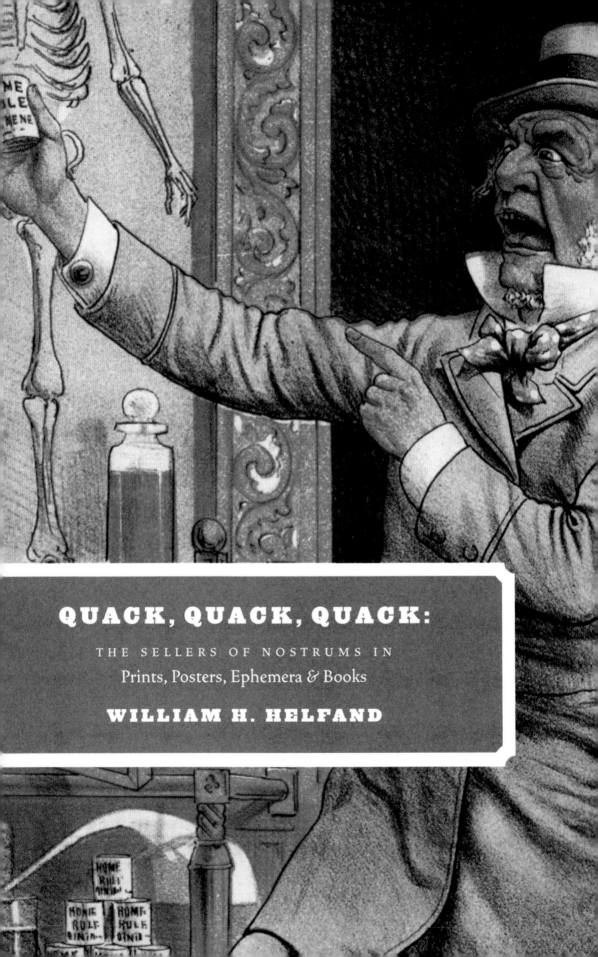

QUACK, QUACK, QUACK:

THE SELLERS OF NOSTRUMS IN
Prints, Posters, Ephemera & Books

WILLIAM H. HELFAND

{ WILLIAM DRENTTEL & JESSICA HELFAND

WINTERHOUSE PRODUCTS

William Drenttel and Jessica Helfand are partners in Winterhouse, a design firm that concentrates on editorial design and the development of new models for old and new media. They are the cofounders of Design Observer, an online design weblog. Winterhouse Editions publishes literature and design criticism. Helfand is a media columnist for Eye and a contributing editor of I.D. magazine. Drenttel serves as creative director for The Poetry Foundation in Chicago and Nextbook in New York.

Did you found Winterhouse to be a design firm serving clients or a firm that designs products of your own creation?

WD: We started working together in 1995 in New York City, and initially the practice was mostly client based. Winterhouse was created as a place to live and work. It is an idea. It does not exist to service clients, even as we do so. But it also does not exist to create products. It exists, on a very personal basis, to integrate our roles as parents, teachers, leaders, designers, publishers, and writers into one place, one life.

Do you have a philosophy about work that now pervades Winterhouse?

WD: I believe strongly that designers have been, for way too long, trying to separate the paying work from the work that mattered; the work they did for publication and awards versus the work they did that paid the rent, and the good work from the bad work. Tibor Kalman used to talk this way—kind of a Robin Hood taking from big, bad, corporate America to pay for the work he really wanted to do. We used to fight about this. Meanwhile, we were ultimately doing the same thing. It took changing the scale of the practice—and making it personal—to fundamentally change the parameters.

JH: Working together has also required a kind of divide-and-conquer approach to life. With clients, with children, with writing, and publishing projects—it sometimes feels like a relay race, with one of us working feverishly to do

something before passing the baton to the other. But I have to say, too, that the other huge shift came for us in living in the country: oddly, after so many years living in cities, we found once we got here that we were more productive, more focused. And that kind of time to think, to reflect, has led to all sorts of other opportunities for making work.

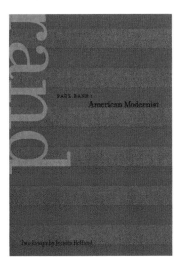

(Left) Book cover for *Quack, Quack, Quack,* a Winterhouse Edition, The Grolier Club, 2002. (Distributed by University of Chicago Press). Designers: William Drenttel, Kevin Smith, and Rob Giampietro.

(Above) *Paul Rand: American Modernist.* Winterhouse Editions, 1998. Designers: Jessica Helfand, Drenttel and Jeffrey Tyson

One of your most "commercial-free" products is the tabloid, *Below the Fold*. What was the impetus for this? And what is your sought-after outcome?

WD: *Below the Fold* grew out of our frustration with publishing—how much it costs, how long it takes, how hard it is to crack the distribution necessary to sell books. We had all these book projects piling up that were never going to see the light of day. Who wants a book on Imre Reiner? But our library and collections are rich, and Below the Fold was conceived as it is named—a place to publish things that fall "below the fold," in the newspaper sense of the word. It is commercial free only because it would take more time to do it to make money. This does not mean we may not grow it into a subscription-based product in the future, but our inclination is to keep it simple. It's something we write, edit, and design that does not have to go through the filter of sales or marketability. It is simply what we make and we mail it to people who ask to receive it. This is not idealism; it is simply the simplest of business models. We make it because we want people to read it. Every practice should have a few such indulgences.

Is self-publishing part of the strategy of your design practice? And do you have an overall business plan?

WD: We believe a design practice can be, and should be, a multifaceted activity. The lines between writing and designing, designing and teaching, designing and publishing, and publishing and research are flexible and ever changing. Adding clients into the mix only makes things more interesting. We are trying to engage with work and ideas that interest us, using the tools of a design practice. It is our practice. It's not about a business plan. It's about wanting to make things, to create new ways of participating in ideas. In this interview, we are primarily talking about books, but this is a fraction of our practice.

In addition to the various book projects, you are cofounders and do the lion's share of maintaining the blog, Design Observer. So another crass

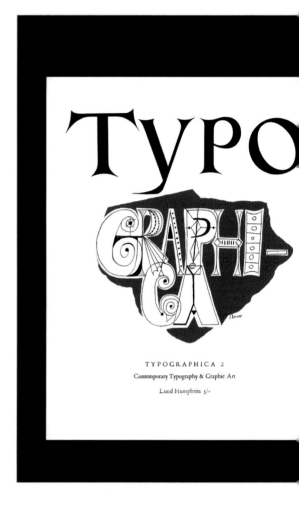

TYPOGRAPHICA 2
Contemporary Typography & Graphic Art
Lund Humphries 5/-

question: Is there more than intellectual profit to be had in this venture?

WD: There will ultimately be financial profit from Design Observer. But it will flow from creating something of quality that large numbers of people come to read. The intellectual profit happens everyday. It is hard work—mundane, detailed, editorial work. Design Observer is five years old. With Michael Bierut, we will have written over 200 essays. But we will have published 50 other writers and another couple of hundred essays. You have to enjoy the making of the site, the engagement with a new writer, the posting of a fresh essay, the daily drama of comments, and spam. Remember, we sustain Design Observer while running full-time practices. This is not a

17

Examples of illustrative words and logotypes.

(Top) The Design Observer homepage an online design forum founded in October 2003 by Michael Bierut, Drenttel, Helfand

hobby. This is not about supporting a small community of readers. Whatever our original ambitions, Design Observer is something larger.

VOLUME 1. NUMBER 1. Literary panoramas. Political stalemates. Historical standards. Material Obsolescence. Topics that fly below the radar yet persist nonetheless, shifting perspectives and sparking debate. This is the purview of Below the Fold: — an occasional publication from the Winterhouse Institute that adapts classic journalistic paradigms through the critical lens of visual inquiry. Where do we turn when leadership is compromised? What do we understand when we look at literary and scientific journals? Why is the human hand so frequently at odds with the man-made? When is photographic evidence a smokescreen for truth? How do we determine directions, distinguish messages, decode the landscape, divine the future? Within the limitations of a printed publication, each issue of Below the Fold: will explore a single topic through visual narrative and critical inquiry, examining ideas that are technically "below the fold" to reveal alternative ways of looking at the world we live in. From a forgotten muralist of the twentieth century, to the media doublespeak of the twenty-first, to the questionable veracity of political jargon, to the visual language of third-world cultures, we will explore the visual permutations of modern life. In this, our premiere issue, we look at the virgin efforts of scholarly journals — an editorial genre perhaps best characterized by its arcane and often impenetrable content. Yet in spite of their extraordinary topical range, what these publications share is an unparalleled idealism, a sense that the future holds nothing but opportunity and promise. — The Editors. SPRING 2006.

(Above) Winterhouse Institute house publication, *Below the Fold*: Imre Reiner Issue (spread). Volume 1: Number 3, Winter 2006. Designers: Drenttel, Helfand and Geoff Halber.

(Right) *Below the Fold:* Collection Issue (cover) Volume 1, Number 1, Spring 2006. Designers: Drenttel, Helfand and Halber

REVISTA GRATUITA DE
CINE Y AUDIOVISUALES
DICIEMBRE 2002 / N°12

SCoPE

: pornografía en el punto de mira
+ Aki Kaurismäki Un hombre sin pasado

Cover of *Scope* magazine
#12. Photo by Guillermo
Merino. Porn Special Issue.
Articles included "How to
do your own porn flicks."
Editor: Marc Prades; creative
director: Jordi Duró; art
director: Violeta Valle.

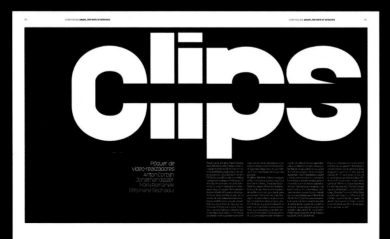

Spread from *Scope* #1.
Lettering by Sandra Bosch
and Duró. Monograph on the
best Music Clip Directors.
Editor: Prades; creative
director: Duró; art director:
Valle.

{ JORDI DURÓ

SCOPE MAGAZINE

J *ordi Duro founded Estudi Duro Communications Solutions in Barcelona in 2001. The firm specializes in corporate and editorial design and creates and communicates brands, using packaging, brochures, or advertising campaigns. He teaches a master's degree course on brand design and corporate identity at Pompeu Fabra University.*

You run a design studio in Barcelona. How did you become the publisher of *Scope*?
A friend introduced Violeta (my wife, who is a newspaper designer) and myself to these two guys—Misha Kominek (a photographer) and Marc Prades (a journalist)—who wanted to do a free cinema magazine. They had both worked on free fashion/lifestyle magazines, which were booming at the time. We all thought new Spanish media outlets were overlooking media and we did a prototype to show to potential advertisers. Misha left the team early, and Violeta and I became very involved, up to the point of investing in it financially and becoming partners with Marc. When the magazine folded after fifteen issues, a film production company that wanted a more lavish "digital lifestyle" approach bought us. They retained the three of us, and because of the bigger budget, we were able to have full time writers, a photo editor, a producer, and so on.

What were some of the unexpected challenges, or problems, once you began publishing?
Although I was familiar with journalism and design, getting a magazine out in the street with a shoestring budget is very intense work. Asking for favors from collaborators was especially hard, as we knew the value of their effort.

***Scope* is a high-quality magazine; it's not cheap to produce. How was the funding handled? Did you have to invest any of your own funds?**
On its first incarnation, we were the main investors. When things started to get bumpy, we were given desks and phones for free by one of Barcelona's top creative ad agencies, SCPF, to do the magazine at their place. They were very supportive and believed in our project. I think they especially liked that we came up with the first Spanish music video festival, VideoClub.

What was the initial reception to the magazine?
Great. People liked the contents. We had good articles about subjects nobody was talking about at the time, such as music clips, digital films, film titles, and so on The up-and-coming young directors we supported are now directing big budget films. Because of the limited budget, we had to cram a lot of information in a very limited space. That's where Violeta's expertise came in and made it very legible. People felt they were getting valuable info for nothing. It didn't feel like your typical free magazine. As a matter of fact, we even had paying subscribers—a paradox for a free magazine.

How did you distribute *Scope*?
In its first incarnation, the magazine was distributed in all the cinemas, libraries, and advertisers' stores in Barcelona, so we had a delivery service do the route. When we would run out of money, we would do it ourselves. In its second incarnation, it was a newsstand magazine, so we picked strategically among the major newsstands throughout Spain with the distributor.

Spread from *Scope* #7. Photo essay on the ubiquity of screens in everyday life. Photos by Guillermo Merino; editor: Prades; creative director: Duró; art director: Valle.

Spread from *Scope* #2 "In the mood for love." Press Photo. Article on the new Hong Kong Cinema. Editor: Prades; creative director: Duró; art director: Valle.

Cover of *Scope* #8 about
"Smoking room" movie,
showing one of the rookie
directors taking a first puff.
Photo: Txema Salvans. Cover
editor: Prades; creative
director: Duró; art director:
Valle.

Obviously, it folded. What were the issues leading up to this?
In its first incarnation, we relied on small advertisers, and we barely pulled through. But when we tried to get campaigns, we learned that agencies planned a year ahead and were suspicious with new magazines due to their high mortality rate. We kept going without a serious income plan, which was a bad idea. Soon enough, we had a bad cash turnaround. Advertisers paid 90 days after publication and we had a couple of big non payers, leaving the magazine without real funding expectations for the next three months. We were exhausted and burned out by then. The second time *Scope* folded, it had nothing to do with the magazine itself. The new owners decided to shut down everything except their film productions.

Do you think you succeeded? How do you define success?
Obviously, we didn't succeed financially. One could even say that we ended up paying for our education. But we also ended up becoming friends with a bunch of talented people with whom we now work on different projects. *Scope* has also been a great introductory card for new clients, a showcase of what we can do apart from mere layout work.

Is there any chance that *Scope* will be revived?
Technology has changed so much in the last seven years that we feel that a paper magazine wouldn't be a fit any longer for audiovisual content. We were the spokespeople of new media, and now it would be feasible to do it online. The team is still there, and there's great stuff to talk about. We just need a new name!

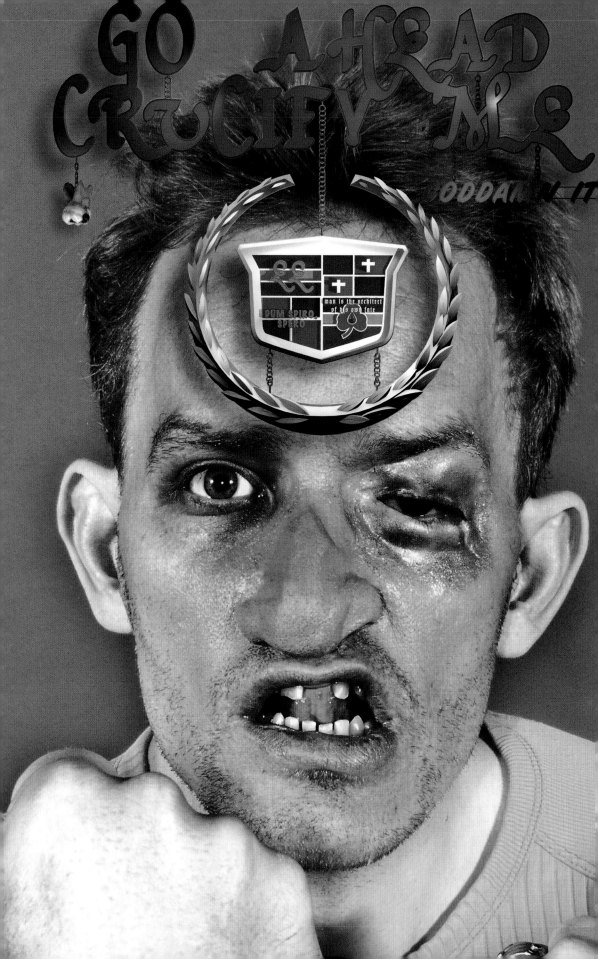

{ ELLIOTT EARLS

THE APOLLO PROGRAM

Elliott Earls is a designer, performance artist, and educator. He is a designer-in-residence at the Cranbrook Academy of Art and head of the graduate two-dimensional design department. For the past fifteen years, Earls has operated a studio dubbed The Apollo Program. His work fuses design principles and methodologies with performance, film, and art-making practice.

(Left) From the *Bull and Wounded Horse* Exhibition, *Go Ahead and Crucify Me, Goddamn it* and (above) *Abraham–N–Isaac* by Elliot Earls.

You design type, you make music, you create performance happenings, and you run a graduate design program at Cranbrook. But are you a design entrepreneur?

Even though I run a graduate studio, the academy supports, encourages, and demands that the department heads have a tangible practice. As a matter of fact, the pedagogical model is based upon this idea. However, I don't maintain an entrepreneurial practice to fulfill a teaching requirement; quite the opposite. My entrepreneurial practice drives my teaching and provides me with whatever "authority" I have as a mentor.

From what I can tell, you've never stuck to the traditional design path.

I'm passionately opposed to the idea of a "traditional design path." This statement requires a bit of clarification. It's my belief that a universal goal of being human is to attempt to find a path through life that allows for a kind of self-actualization. One of the most important projects that I have been working on in my studio over the course of the past year is a feature-length, high-definition, digital film entitled, *The Saranay Motel.* This film is essentially a rags-to-riches-to-rags story tracing the career of two of Detroit's least-talented hip-hop artists. Of course, while I wrote, directed, scored, and am editing the film, it is by far the most ensemble project I have worked on. My point is that, in this process, I take great pleasure in designing the graphic language for the film.

But why become a designer in the first place?
Because of the connection to media and commerce, I find the completely artificial and fallacious distinction between "commercial" and "fine art" to be a particularly onerous cultural construction. I want to actively engage issues of branding, marketing, advertising, and graphic language in a substantive body of artwork. I also want to sell the work. And on this point, I'd like to be perfectly clear. My goal is to make work that is a form of cultural criticism, that at times is a biting form of satire, and that finds its place in relationship to a community (an audience). These goals seem to me to be consistent with a hybrid form that draws as much from graphic design as it does art practice.

When you started designing type, back in the days of grunge, when the early fontographer programs made it easy to do on the desktop, were you making art or commerce?
It's fairly obvious that the typefaces that I have designed are idiosyncratic, to say the least. They lie at the core of my aesthetic. This issue addresses your last question as well. Because I design my typefaces as an essential building block of my aesthetic, I'm not really interested in other people using them. There are a few exceptions, Calvino Hand and Venus Dioxide, for example. I was very interested in the commercial aspects of fonts, but only in the most pragmatic sense. I realized that if I began selling my fonts, they would be pirated and spread all over planet earth. That is what I wanted. I also wanted

Selection from Émigré presents the *Typography of Elliott Earls'*. The booklet was designed by Earls and featured a collection of original typeface designs.

Portrait of a *Young Man*, Busts in clay and bronze by Earls.

Emigre's marketing muscle and brand cache to benefit me. So as a strategy I named each of the fonts distributed through Emigre "Elliott's … blah blah blah," with the understanding that soon most designers would have my name in their font menu. Emigre's marketing muscle benefited me enormously. My typefaces were pirated and my career profile was raised.

How does graphic design fit into your overall, grand plan for making art?
Graphic design lies at the core of my grand-master-super-secret-plan. I'm serious. Look, it's clear that I consider myself a graphic designer and an artist. But graphic design is my secret weapon.

Have you considered selling your wares in a mainstream sort of way?
I have considered it. But to be honest, I think my work has confounded categorization a bit too handily. I am very interested in seeing my work in relationship to a larger audience. My larger goal has always been to cultivate an audience. Selling my wares in a more mainstream way would be good.

What has been your most challenging entrepreneurial product(s) and why?
I would say the piece that I am currently working on poses the greatest challenges. I have filmed over 750 gigabytes of footage in a variety of formats ranging from mini-DVDs to DVCPRO HD. This is unequivocally my most challenging entrepreneurial product because I feel as if this project has the potential to bring together my vision in a very powerful way. Why is it challenging? Well, there are the structural issues. I wrote, directed, acted, scored, edited, branded, and produced the project. But the larger issue is one of audience. Your previous question about the importance of audience is an arrow through the heart of this project. Films are meant to be viewed.

Part narrative film, part documentary, *Catfish* is a fifty-five minute digital film incorporating; motion graphics, typography, and animation into a kind of experimental film.

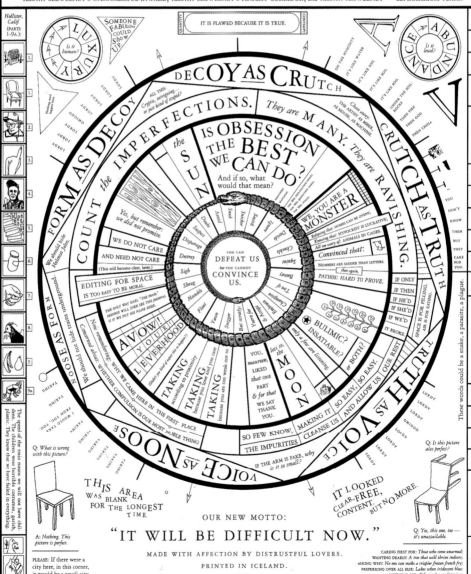

{ DAVE EGGERS
McSWEENEY'S PUBLISHING

D*ave Eggers, founder of McSweeney's Publishing, is a writer and designer. His first magazine,* Might, *was founded in 1999. He has designed most of the books and quarterlies published by McSweeney's. In 2003, his designs for McSweeney's were featured in the National Design Triennial at the Cooper-Hewitt National Design Museum. He is the author of the novel,* You Shall Know Our Velocity *(2002) and the memoir,* A Heartbreaking Work of Staggering Genius *(2000), among other books.*

McSweeney's is a literary journal founded and originally designed by Dave Eggers. While it retains its own integral audience, it is also the hub of other entrepreneurial ventures, including a website, book division, and stores that cater to the eccentric and unusual aspects of visual and literary culture. *McSweeney's* No. 1, 2 (1998), and 3 (1999), designed by Eggers, is a literary journal for "generation I"—the irony generation.

You studied painting. You worked at designing. You wrote an incredibly successful memoir about you and your brother. You started a literary journal and website that touched a cross-generational nerve. And you have started seven quirky stores called 826 in San Francisco, Los Angeles, Chicago, Seattle, Ann Arbor, New York, and soon Boston that offer inspiration and outreach to kids ages eight to eighteen. How did McSweeney's come about and blossom into so many other endeavors?

McSweeney's began in 1998 with the website, followed a few months later by the first journal. There were a bunch of reasons I started it. First, I was stalling on my first book and I needed something tangible to work on. I was working at *Esquire* at the time and that didn't feel tangible much of the time. I was getting very few of my ideas into print, so I had a lot of excess energy, lots of ideas that were dying on the vine. At first, *McSweeney's* was really a reaction against big-budget, glossy magazines in that it was incredibly simple and it published things that had been killed by mainstream magazines. When I published the first issue, and then the second, I really liked the simplicity of the process, where someone would send me a story, I'd typeset it, and it would get published—in sharp contrast to working at a company where, for example, we had to fill out a form to send one letter (true story). I guess I got spoiled working for alternative weeklies and then starting

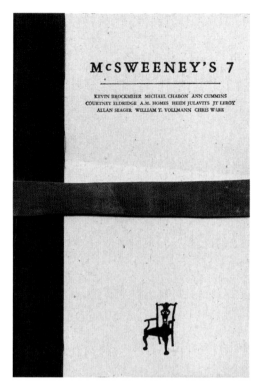

McSweeney's No. 9 (2002), designed by Eggers, riffs on the conventional literary journal conventions with a collection of jumbled typographical headlines.

McSweeney's No. 7 (2001) is a classic paper and cloth binding with letterpress cover type. The contents are, however, loosely held together by an industrial rubber band.

little magazines like *Might*. I got hooked on the smaller-scale projects where you could just think of an idea and then it would be in print a week or so later.

So how did this evolve into a veritable empire?
When you begin a little thing like McSweeney's, you start attracting and otherwise getting into contact with a lot of creative people, refugees from more restrictive jobs and situations. So then you all start dreaming up other random ideas. That's how the McSweeney's store began in Park Slope in Brooklyn, New York. Scott Seeley, who was originally a McSweeney's intern, helped build this very weird place on 7th Avenue that sold taxidermy supplies and show-animal grooming supplies and books like *Caring for Your Miniature Donkey*. We'd both wanted to run a

useless curiosity shop, and that was fun, but of course it lost money.

Around the second year of the store, we moved back to San Francisco and rented the space at 826 Valencia. And though the landlord was open to our running an educational nonprofit there, he insisted we sell something in the front. The street is zoned for retail, so we had to think of something. That's why the pirate store happened. It was an idea that made me laugh, so that was that. I don't usually overthink something like that. I thought that would be the most absurd way possible of fulfilling the retail obligation. So we opened the store, and incredibly, it did well. It paid the rent. And it brought in tons of foot traffic. And that foot traffic led to the students, their parents, the teachers, donors, and volunteers.

McSweeney's No. 17 (2005) is a collection of separate booklets and other printed ephemera that approximates everyday junk mail

Thus the retail part of the plan became part of the 826 model. After that, the growth happened very organically. Scott Seeley and the rest of the people who had worked at the Brooklyn taxidermy shop wanted to start an 826 there, so they rented a new space and that became 826NYC and the Brooklyn Superhero Supply Company. That led another friend in Los Angeles to begin 826LA and on and on. Local writers and teachers who wanted to replicate the model started all of the locations and put their own twist on it.

It has lasted for so long. I presume there wasn't a longevity plan?
I never thought any of this would happen. That is, I never look that far forward, for better or worse. *McSweeney's*

was supposed to go eight issues and then fold. It wasn't supposed to tendril out to the *Believer* and *Wholphin* and all that. But more people came along who helped some of these unrealistic ideas become plausible. The same thing happened with 826. It was supposed to be one simple neighborhood center doing one thing—after-school tutoring. But then hundreds of tutors showed up and that made a dozen other things possible: field trips, evening workshops, dozens of publications, in-school tutoring, a summer camp, and so on.

I think the main factor to the success is our organization's openness to new things and to allowing our staff to take things in new directions.

McSweeney's is not only a publishing empire (I'm reminded somehow of *Rolling Stone's* Straight Arrow Publishing), but also an impressive brand, as in seal of approval for a generation of literati. Much of the physical manifestation is thanks to your design sensibility. How would you define that sensibility?
Well, some aspects of the sensibility have definitely been evolving. At first, it was more rigid; for about six years, I designed almost all of the books and journals myself, and I kept the look fairly constrained. I wanted the design to be unobtrusive, given I had spent a lot of time in glossy magazines, and wanted a more stripped-down sensibility. And separately, I wanted to see how much could be done with just one font, so almost every McSweeney's book and journal for maybe six years used Garamond 3. After that, though, we started expanding a bit and now the journal experiments with different looks (while still only using serif fonts and Garamond 3 for all the interior text). There's still a concentration on detail and a preference for a handcrafted look as opposed to anything too modern or clean or streamlined. I think the prose we publish, which is usually of a slightly offbeat nature, demands a handcrafted look. That means a lot of illustration (as opposed to photos) and a kind of obsession with odd details, while also maintaining an openness to some rough edges, some happy accidents. I think books are very tactile and personal

> I think the main factor to the success is our organization's openness to new things and to allowing our staff to take things in new directions.

things, so it feels good to me, at least, when they're created with a personal touch, even if that means they're as quirky and flawed as the people who make them.

Do you believe you've established an infrastructure that could continue even without your influential input?
It does already. I have to write my own books and tour when a new book comes out, and I need to be home with my family, so I can't be in the office every day. As a result, every *McSweeney's* entity is fairly self-sufficient and autonomous. *The Believer*, in particular, is published ten times a year without much influence from me at all. All I do is look through the proofs and mark a few things. In terms of *McSweeney's* as a journal, we have it split up at this point whereby Eli Horowitz, our editor/publisher, edits and conceives of two issues a year, and I conceive and edit the other two. And all of the issues are ushered through by Jordan Bass, our managing editor (there are only three of us working on the editorial side). So these days, I don't have to do all that much of the heavy lifting on any given entity. The same goes for the books; I bring in and edit some of the books we publish, and Eli brings in and edits more of them these days. The website, too, is pretty much autonomous, edited by John Warner out of his home in West Virginia. We e-mail each other pretty much every day, but I don't see what he's going to publish until the public sees it.

Let's talk about the *McSweeney's* style. You always make the journal different. I never know when I open my mail subscription package what I will find—a cigar box of ephemera, a collection of small pamphlets, a mix of ersatz junk mail, or a gorgeously produced book with neo-rococo illustrations. What is the rationale behind this?
With every issue, we honestly first sit down and think about a format we haven't used yet. Sometimes this is based on something we've seen before—a technique or look that hasn't been seen in a long time. That was the case with Issue 11, when we started using foil

McSweeney's No. 19 follows the form of a traditional cigar box. The contents are variously sized booklets of stories and graphics.

McSweeney's No. 20 (2006) is a traditional paper over boards cover with a gouache painting by Jacob Magraw-Mickleson overprinting and obliterating the editorial on the front.

Thrilling Tales, edited by Michael Chabon, is a McSweeney's book of fiction with a cover designed in the style of 1930s pulp magazines

stamps a lot. I couldn't believe how beautiful the metallic stamping could look and how seldom it was used outside of encyclopedias. Sometimes it's just a new and random idea. The cigar box issue came about when I drove by a cigar store that was giving away cigar boxes. I stopped, took some home, started experimenting a bit with them, and thought it might make a good package concept. The goal is to always surprise the readers and bring them true tactile delight. We want a subscriber to actually experience delight—as corny a word as that is—when they open their quarterly package. Most of our work is in trying to find and publish the very best stories and essays that we can possibly find, but the surprise of the form is really key to us, too.

Obviously, the McSweeney's store is a destination for the odd gift. How often do you develop new products? On your website, you sell bundles of magazines, paper goods, and T-shirts. Do you simply produce what strikes your fancy or is there a method to the madness?

I wish I could say there was more of a method, but it's 98 percent random. No one at McSweeney's had any formal training in publishing, marketing, anything. Almost everyone on the staff came up through the intern ranks, so they've all been learning as they go. Heidi Meredith manages the website store and she's the most in touch with what people are ordering. But there's very little science to it. We're a pretty disorganized bunch and there are only six staff members. So even when we say, which we often do, "Okay, we have to start really doing this, or doing that"—for example, things that might make some money—we rarely can do many of those things, because there isn't enough time, capital, or staff. But when we do something new, something in the gift realm, it usually works like this: At a staff meeting, someone might say, "Hey, what about posters?" Then someone else will call around and see how much posters cost to make. If we find out they're affordable, we do a poster, like the *Believer* poster we did a little while ago. Then of course, we find out that though the poster is quite beautiful—designed by our own Alvaro Villanueva using Charles Burns' astounding portraits—it doesn't really sell very well. So we don't do more posters. That's the A to Z of our scientific method.

I'm dying to ask if you make a profit on these things?
Certain things make a profit while others lose money. Overall, we've been losing a certain dependable amount of money for the last seven years or so. Had we been better at numbers, and deadlines, we probably wouldn't have lost much money at all. But again, we all learned this on the job and we made more mistakes than could be counted or believed. And then, of course, our distributor went bankrupt. We lost a lot of money there. But things are getting better. We're getting better at the math-and-projections side of the business all the time.

***The Believer* has garnered a terrific reputation in large part because it is a very literate and eclectic publication. Moreover, it has such an unambiguous identity, almost nineteenth century in its typographic charms. How did you decide on this look?**
I was first just trying to make a magazine that didn't look much like anything else out there. So I started with the almost-square format, a look I've always liked. Then I realized that no magazine I'd seen had done a full-bleed color border, so that became part of it. After that, I had to create a template that could be easily maintained. I knew that the magazine would have to have a small staff,

because we started with a $12,000 investment and didn't want to take advertising. So I did some math with Barb and we figured that we could pay one full-time staff member and three part-timers. The task then was to design the magazine in a way that could be maintained by the one full-time managing editor, Andrew Leland.

I should emphasize something that a lot us who started in zines have known for a while, which is that you don't need a staff of 100 to put out a magazine, even a monthly magazine with as much text as *The Believer* has. Especially if the editors, like Andrew, can do a lot of things—design, correct photos, commission artwork, write headlines—then your staff doesn't need to be huge and doesn't need to be divided along the traditional art/editorial lines (lines I think need to be blurred). If you can keep staff costs lean, then you can put out very idiosyncratic magazines with little or no advertising. We tried to figure out the minimum amount of subscribers we'd need to make the thing work and then budgeted from there.

The Believer, illustrated by Charles Burns, is a monthly book review and literary journal printed on calendared beige paper stock. Unlike *McSweeney's*, it retains a rather consistent style and publishing schedule.

{ BARBARA ENSOR

LITTLE SCHOOL OF MOVING PICTURES

Barbara Ensor is an illustrator and children's book author. She has written for numerous publications including New York *magazine,* Entertainment Weekly, and the Village Voice. *Her illustrations have appeared in the* New York Times, Harper's Magazine, Self, *and* Graphis, *among others.*

You began as an illustrator and transformed into a business that teaches young kids to make claymation films. How come?

I always liked clay animation, and a couple of years ago I stumbled onto the fact that stop-motion animation is really quick and cheap now. All you need is a digital camera and some relatively simple software. I was working in a high school where the kids had persuaded the administration to let them have a class in clay animation. Then I volunteered to teach a free clay animation class to kids at the Super Hero Supply Store in Brooklyn, New York, created by Dave Eggers and McSweeney's.

Were you a seasoned claymationateer?

I was worried I wouldn't be able to deliver. I kept repeating, "We'll see what happens," in the first session. But thanks to a bunch of terrific adult volunteers (one was an accomplished film-maker, another had been a help line person at Apple), we had a great time and made a voice we were all proud of. The more I caught up on the technical end of it, the more clearly I could see that this wasn't really about that. It comes down to storytelling, as well as playing well together.

How do you go about getting students?

Right now, I leave postcards around the neighborhood and occasionally a parent will wander onto my website and send me an e-mail. Usually, the person that does sign up their child for class has had a personal connection, either to me or to clay animation in general. But then the

Claymation figure by Barbara Ensor for the *Little School of Moving Pictures.*

snowball starts to grow because friends want to sign up too. Once classes begin, the publicity engine really heats up.

What do you really offer the students? What are the outcomes other than the screening?

We can all take it for granted that this generation will be making movies without help from me or anyone else. An awful lot of them already are. I have my aesthetic agenda. For example, I like to promote the tactile quality of clay and crumpled paper bags over computer generated stuff, which to me is completely boring. And I also like to encourage real storytelling over empty technical pizzazz. I am in the business of raising these kids' media literacy a notch.

You've originated children's books. Is there a relationship between the books and films?
A lot is similar. Getting the pacing right, paring it down to the essential conflicts, and so forth are comparable. But of course, when I make movies, I am not in charge. I am running alongside and occasionally waving my arms around. With books, I do the words, and the pictures, and rely on my editor to wave the arms around.

Well, do you have any kind of viable business model or is this just a seat-of-the-pants entrepreneurship?
I kind of have a vision I hold onto at the core of it, and I reckon there's a viable long-term business in there. I am talking to a couple of nonprofits about using sections of the movies made with kids and wrapping them up in a different way in order to raise funds and promote knowledge about their institutions. So long as it does not bog us down, that kind of dual-purpose approach, where we provide content as well as teaching, could open up other sources of funding besides tuition.

(Above) Screenshot from littleschoolofmovingpictures.com and (below) promotional postcard used to attract students to the school. Designer: Ensor.

{ SHEPARD FAIREY

STUDIO NUMBER ONE

S *hepard Fairey is a designer and illustrator who founded Studio Number One in Los Angeles and is publisher of* Swindle *magazine. But he is best known for having revived the images of Andre the Giant, a has-been wrestler, transforming his scowling face and the word "Obey" into a logo of youthful defiance against everything the previous generation held dear. Today, he's a brand, "a trademark of alienation," and has been copied by marketers, yet he is also the figurehead of street artists and culture-jammers around the world.*

From Obey the Giant to Obey Records, *Swindle,* **and all your other entrepreneurial ventures, did you plan for this business to take off?**

My goal was always to figure out a way to make enough money to survive doing the things I wanted to do on my own terms. When I started making Giant stickers and stencils, I made a few T-shirts to fund the stickers. My background is skateboarding and punk rock, cultures whose proponents primarily identified themselves with T-shirts. It came naturally to me to put my graphics (I did not dare call it art) on T-shirts. Later, as I started making posters to put up on the street, I figured I'd also make some on nicer paper to sell. The sales of the T-shirts, stickers, and posters were a by-product of the impact of the street art, but the street art was not marketing for the products; conversely the products were a way to fund the street art. I also started a screen-printing business while still at RISD (Rhode Island School of Design) so that when I graduated, there would be no lapse in my poster, sticker, and T-shirt production. When I was losing money as a

screen printer, I switched to graphic design as a profession so that I could make a living using my art skills.

Isn't it kind of ironic that Obey, which began as a commentary on consumption and the tools of persuasion, has become such a persuasive brand?

I can see the irony there, but it is important to understand that Obey was never intended to destroy capitalism or conspicuous consumption, but to make people more aware of their manipulative influence. I feel that a lot of the messages from Obey encourage people to question

(Left) "Do As He Says Not as He Does" political poster by Shepard Fairey, and (right) cover for his pop culture magazine *Swindle*, published by Studio Number One.

things. Of course, there are always trendy people who latch onto things for the wrong reasons; that is inevitable. However, there is the possibility for a bandwagon jumper to be enlightened once they discover the history of the project. Is wearing an "I Hate Fashion" T-shirt a fashion or antifashion statement? I named my book *Supply and Demand* as an acknowledgment of some of the complexities of commenting on and participating in capitalism simultaneously.

As quickly as you release a poster, another is out. What determines what you will publish? Do you have an agenda?
I make art all the time. When I feel a poster is resolved, I print it. I try to release a new poster every week. I'm trying to find the best balance of quantity and quality, maintaining an awareness of the fickle nature and rapid metabolism of consumer culture. My agenda is simply to make art that is visually stimulating enough at a glance for people to care. Additionally, I have a point of view about many topics that is addressed in most of the work. If nothing else, I hope my work combats complacency by demonstrating how easy it is to make, disseminate, and sell stuff. I'm into empowering people.

Stylistically, your work runs the gamut of revolutionary to Victorian, a wonderful marriage of stark modernism and decorative eclecticism. How do you define the style?
My style started to become distinctive about 12 years ago. I was heavily influenced by Russian Constructivism. As time has gone on, I have kept the limited color palette of propaganda art, but I've brought in more decorative elements including patterns and a softer Art Nouveau

Series of Obey posters by Fairey which are sold via his website and illegally posted on city streets. (Far right) Lollapalooza poster promoting the rock concert.

influence. I think I wanted to give my work more layers, but keep it bold. The Nouveau influence is partially conceptual because the hippies borrowed from Nouveau and I have been promoting peace with my work. I'm a design mutt. My influences range from punk album sleeves to currency design. Consistent color theory is a remarkably reliable unifying technique.

In truth, how successful have your products been? And do you base your decisions on that measure of success or on your passion for doing it?
My products have been successful enough for me to make a decent living for my family. I make enough to have the freedom to work on projects I want to work on and turn the others down. In the art and design world, that is a minor miracle and I think that is a much more important success than anything that could be measured materially.

> When I feel a poster is resolved, I print it. I try to release a new poster every week. I'm trying to find the best balance of quantity and quality...

{ LOUISE FILI

A DESIGNER'S GUIDE TO ITALY

*L*ouise Fili, proprietor of Louise Fili Ltd. in New York, specializes in food packaging, logos, restaurant, and book design. She is the coauthor of many books on art deco and author of The Civilized Shopper's Guide to Florence. *Her work is in the permanent collections of the Library of Congress, the Cooper Hewitt Museum, and the Bibliotheque Nationale.*

What was your first entrepreneurial product?
I made (and designed the label for) my own basil vinegar.

Did it succeed or fail?
It succeeded in that I produced a couple hundred bottles, which were sold in one specialty market in Manhattan. However, one season of a cottage industry was more than enough to send me hightailing it back to the cushy world of graphic design.

Other than running your own design business, what did you have to learn to become a design entrepreneur?
Before you do anything, you must be aware of all the things that can go wrong, who can sue you (this is the food industry, remember), and of course, you need to know all of the legal requirements.

Your guide to Italy is obviously the result of your passions. What was your aim in doing this book?
For years and years, I would field calls from people who would say, "You don't know me, but I am going to Italy and I hear that you know all the cool places that a graphic designer would like." It started with stacks of pages that I would fax according to this stranger's itinerary. Then it turned to e-mail. Finally, I thought it would be fun to put it all into a little limited-edition book. It is my love letter to Italy.

Was profit anywhere in the picture?
No. Profit was never in the big picture.

You saw this as the first of a series. What happened?
The plan was to do Paris next. I still expect to do it, but other projects have gotten in the way.

After designing thousands of books and coauthoring a few, you've become the sole author, designer, and photographer for a guidebook to Florence. What are some of the challenges you had to face with this?

I had never written a book before, and I quickly learned that this requires a side of the brain that I do not normally use. I planned two trips to Florence to work on the book, which meant that I had to be extremely organized and do a great deal of preliminary research beforehand. Once there, I visited an average of 10 shops a day, where I needed to interview the owner in Italian; fact-check the address, phone number, hours of operation, and so on, mark the location on the map; and take digital photos. In the evenings, I would eat in restaurants that I needed to review for the book, and once back at my hotel, I would edit my notes (which were half in English, half in Italian) and make a to-do list for the next day. Back in New York, I wrote and designed the book over the course of a few months.

Your publisher also released a box of cards you created of antique buttons. How much of your entrepreneurial work is rooted in your personal interests?

My work tends to be very personal, and I purposely maintain a small studio so that I can focus on projects that interest me.

What did you already know about publishing that prepared you for your own publishing venture?

After decades of having to read so many bad manuscripts, I would hope that my tenure in publishing taught me something about writing. Also, schedules were so ingrained in me that I didn't dare miss a deadline.

Do you see more entrepreneurial projects in the future?

Of course. Any excuse to go to Italy!

(Left) Cover and spread of Italian shop and beach club signs (right) from *A Designer's Guide to Italy*, look at the boot through the lens of design excellence. Designers: Louise Fili and MaryJane Callister; art director: Fili.

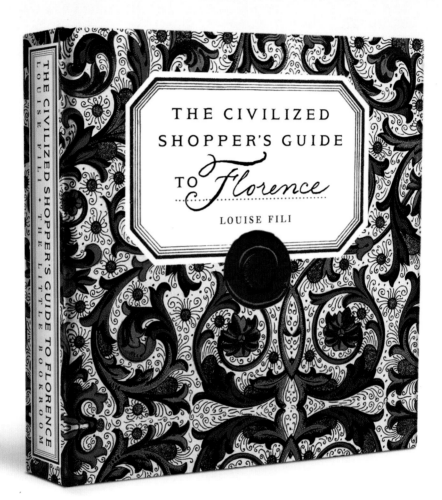

Cover for A Shoppper's Guide to Florence by Fili, surveying the best places in Florence to spend Euros. Designer and photographer: Fili.

Spreads of orange wrappers
and newspaper pages from
A Designer's Guide to Italy.
Designers: Fili and Callister;
Art Director: Fili.

{ KARIN HIBMA

WALKING MAN

*K*arin Hibma is a founding partner in Cronan, a design firm focused on naming and strategic brand identities. Clients include Amazon, Apple, Estée Lauder, the San Francisco Museum of Modern Art, and many Silicon Valley companies. She is also the managing partner of Walking Man, a fashion company whose products are designed by her husband, Michael Patrick Cronan.

When did you start Walking Man?

The very beginning was in 1987, when my husband Michael Cronan and a Cronan Design client began discussing developing a line of men's clothing with innovative design and durable, high-quality fibers and fabrics. Our au pair, a fashion design student, sewed the first prototypes. The first photographs were published in a *Communication Arts* profile of Cronan Design the following year.

And why did you call it that?

Michael had designed a poster for the Stanford Design Conference featuring Japanese design icons, one of which we called the "Walking Man." That icon became our protagonist, the character that went out and explored the world. Walking Man was a good brand name for a product designed for being "at home wherever you are."

What is your background that you decided to concentrate on a fashion line?

Cronan Design's first client was Levi Strauss & Co. Ten-plus years of helping launch product lines for Levi's and other design clients gave us the crazy idea that if you created a great product, marketed it cleverly, and provided great customer service, you could always find customers for your product.

What differentiated you from the outset from other clothing businesses?

Being both an accomplished design firm and a new clothing company worked to differentiate us in many ways, but overall, the biggest impact came from great products and marketing that engaged our customers and wonderful customer service that made them feel the passion and power of the Walking Man identity. Not many clothing companies other than jeans and suit manufacturers were creating a new design lifestyle for men. Walking Man clothing was designed to be an environment; clothing you could put on, travel great distances in, and arrive looking comfortable and appropriate for a meeting or an evening out.

How did you promote Walking Man?

The San Francisco Chronicle ran a full front-page "Lifestyles" article on Father's Day to report on the launch of Walking Man. The feature was about the intersection between our design practice and the clothing. *Graphis*, *ID*, and *Metropolis* magazines, as well as the *New York Observer*, *The New Yorker*, and other publications, worked with us to maximize our limited advertising budget in exchange for creative ads that brought attention to both Walking Man and the publications.

What did you have to learn that was most challenging to enter into this difficult field of retailing?

The business culture is different. The first order we placed for knit fabric for the Urban Uniforms was bought off the looms by a larger clothing company (Esprit), and we were told our order would be replaced when a new shipment of yarn arrived. It set us back, both schedule wise and psychologically. A printer would never treat a graphic designer that way! And designing clothing is not at all like designing an annual report. The customers are individuals; "everybody is perfect," except not every body is the same size: tall and thin, tall and round, smaller than our smallest size, and women who feel totally comfortable wearing clothing designed for men. There is a science to good retailing business; we were experienced with the art and creativity, but we had to learn a lot about the science.

How did you apportion the business? Who designs? Who markets? Who does what?

Michael created the original clothing designs. After two other business relationships failed, I created Cronan Artefact in 1991 to manufacture and market the clothing, and commissioned Michael and Cronan Design to create the Walking Man product identity and graphics. Vicki Küng, an experienced "garmento" who was our "science officer," helped us figure out how to translate drawings into clothing. She later designed uniforms for the Olympics in Atlanta for Primo Angeli's design group. The team of designers at Cronan Design all created graphic themes for us. Our design colleagues offered design input and are some of our best customers. I created the business and marketing strategy, as well as the Legendary shirts, and Küng has several new product designs in prototype.

Can you make a correlation between the fashion and graphic design businesses?

The easy correlation is the ability to make an impact. Design can distill and represent the essence of an idea, while it can also give identifiable form to a large collection of ideas. Graphic designers are hired to make an impact. While we don't consider Walking Man "fashion," our clothing creates, first of all, an environment for the wearer, and secondly, a statement of the wearer's identity within the environment. The business correlation between fashion/clothing and graphic design is one of timeliness and intention, understanding the market and finding opportunities.

How has Walking Man influenced the graphic end of the business?

Walking Man's need for direct mail materials over the first ten years made us be a large client of ourselves and gave us tremendous opportunity to try new ideas, test, experiment, and challenge ourselves, both with our opportunities and with our limitations. We were one of the first online catalogs marketing clothing, and we used the Web to replace the time and material resource-intensive direct marketing. Having made many complex and difficult business decisions for our own product line has made us much more strategic working with our design clients. Developing and marketing our own brand has given us, along with thirty-plus years of design experience, a strength in developing and marketing client's brands.

(Above left) Pants from the Urban Travelers line. Photography: Penning Measles. (Above) Hero Jacket and (left) an assortment of Walking Man print pieces from the fashion catalog. Design: Michael Patrick Cronan; photography: Terry Lorant.

{ NAT HUNTER

AIRSIDE PRODUCTS

*N*at Hunter is cofounder of London-based Airside, founded in 1998 in Islington, London. Her graphic design company is known for stylized animation and illustration. She codesigned the interface for the Jupiter II spaceship in the movie Lost in Space and did performance installation work for Blast Theory before starting Airside.

When did you start doing entrepreneurial work?
Airside has always done self-initiated work. We started with T-shirts and club nights and have recently done art installations and short films.

What brought you and your partners in Airside together?
The thing that united the three of us was that we all thought about the experience of a person. How did they feel when they walked into a club/building/installation or turned on a computer/looked at a website? How could we improve that experience? How could we make people happy and engaged with that experience?

How did the Airside products come about?
We've always used them as a place to experiment and have complete creative freedom. We realized that they might have a wider appeal, so we put them online.

How have these succeeded in the marketplace?
They've consistently sold over the nine years we've been in business. We've never advertised them or marketed them in any way. We've just let them do their own thing.

What would you say is your most successful toy product and how do you measure this success?
Battle Royale has sold the most, but people seem to engage very deeply with the Stitches, which makes

us happy. Battle Royale is a Japanese film distributed by Metro Tartan. They asked us to think about possible marketing material and the tees are still selling to this day.

The Stitches [toys] first came to life in 2001. I was inspired after returning from a trip to Tokyo, where I had seen some fantastically odd knitted things. They would appear in my garden, behind the garden shed, damaged,

vulnerable, and slightly broken, physically and emotionally. So I took them in, looked after them, and rehabilitated them. Airside was having an exhibition at a gallery when the Stitches were first being adopted, so I was lucky enough to meet the new parents. This encouraged them to stay in touch with Airside, sending photos and updates of how their new children were doing in their homes. The advent of blogging has made this even easier, and many Stitches have their own blogs. They are currently adopted out via Airside's online portal, www.airsideshop.com, and frequently appear at exhibitions and events such as Pictoplasma in Berlin. The next step is Podcasts for parents to see how other Stitches are. In 2004, we made a film about the Stitches meeting a gang of leather boys and the ensuing wool bath. It's important to note that no Stitches were harmed in the making of the film.

(Left and above right) Figures, *Dr. Dance*, *Daisy*, *The Thing*, *Simon*, and *Xavier* from Airside's Dot Com Refugees toy collection.

(Right) The Lemon Jelly CD kit with posters and postcards included by Airside.

{ JEFFREY K. JOHNSON

SPUNK DESIGN MACHINE

J*effrey K. Johnson is founder and creative director of Spunk Design Machine in Minneapolis, Minnesota. The studio creates identity systems, books, interiors, packaging, and posters. Spunk has manufactured and sold educational products for kids and designed fonts and products.*

You've called design entrepreneurship a "genetic handicap." Please explain?

The designers I know that have made the leap from traditional graphic design to entrepreneurial design all seem compelled to do so. You can never really get to scratch that particular itch if you don't have the motivation—not until you give it a go. I've watched my colleagues and design heroes like Joe Duffy, Chuck Anderson, Mike Cina, Chank, and so on, experiment, fail, succeed, fail, and succeed again with the new products they author and launch. I've seen this happen over the course of decades. This compulsion to create defies the financial reward and the sound business advice I'm sure they all receive. It betrays a higher motivation that I can only akin to a genetic handicap. It is burned in the DNA.

What were your initial forays into Spunk?

At first it was fonts; I was part of a larger wave of digital type designers that were long on typographic ambition and short on typographic discipline. I soon realized that the products I really want to author should be really grafted to my best hopes and dreams. This led me to author board games for at-risk kids, coloring pages for handicapped kids, and learning tools for autistic kids. The risk involved in any entrepreneurial endeavor is large. It's mitigated when the product you are making has larger social implications.

Has this process of producing without clients helped or hindered your client work?

It's been a win-win. If anything, my product work has

been a great magnet for the leaders, inventors, and entrepreneurs that employ Spunk.

Let's talk about your entrepreneurial projects. What's your favorite and why?

I have to split the difference here and choose two. Talking Tools is certainly the biggest success in terms of creating a product that directly serves to improve the mental wellness of at-risk kids. It's also a consistent money earner, which is important for the long-term goals of an inventor. But more recently, I have to point to my Minnehotrod invention for immediately improving my life in terms of physical fitness and zero carbon emission. The Minnehotrod is a canoe/bike combination that allows me to seamlessly bike my canoe upstream from my watery Minneapolis home and then canoe back. Since inventing this product, I've lost 60 pounds, and six months ago I gave up my truck, so my bike is now my sole transportation source. This has also had a domino effect on my company, in that we now use a car-sharing service in Minneapolis called HourCar that rents cars by the hour. So with one simple invention I've redesigned a big part of my recreational and working lives for the better. Who'da thunk it?

How much of your studio is devoted to entrepreneurial endeavors?

I'd have to say it's about 25 percent of our endeavors if you balanced it out over the last 11 years. It's always a case of overlapping timelines, with client work taking the priority position, as it is always more time sensitive. This approach also gives us the luxury of doing the entrepreneurial work on our terms and within our chosen timeline.

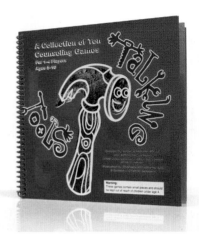

Is there a firm business model on which you build or is this all seat-of-the-pants?
I think all entrepreneurship is a seat-of-the-pants endeavor. But certainly, if you looked at the business model of Charles and Ray Eames, you could draw several lifetimes of lessons. To my satisfaction, there has yet to be an example of invention and design discipline that matches this model.

Why are you called Spunk?
The woman with whom I cofounded Spunk is named Angee Hagen. She's the real reason Spunk started at all. She and I were living with her then-boyfriend, now her husband, Chad Hagen. Angee is an outstanding sculptor and furniture designer. She and I began building crap in our apartment to the gross dissatisfaction of Chad. We eventually rented a studio space and began the first version of our studio together. It was a partnership that lasted for seven years before she became a full-time mom. Angee, Chad, and I are all from the Fargo area. Frequently, we'd travel the four-hour trip back home. On one such trip while building the shop, Angee and her grandmother Mavis were crossing the halfway point of the trip delineated by the Middle Spunk Creek. Mavis offered up that we should name our studio "Spunk" since we were both such spunk kids. We've been Spunk ever since. Looking back on it, being named after a river is a fitting metaphor for this kind of shop. Constant motion, dry times, flood times, sometimes we even switch our banks, but we always move forward. What choice do we really have?

Games designed by Spunk include Talking Tools: A collection of ten counseling board games for ages 5-10 (top) Hospital Pals, a fun and fast board game designed to get young children comfortable with that first trip to the hospital (middle), and Fishing For Feelings, a lighthearted game designed to get kids comfortable with talking about difficult feelings under the safe umbrella of game play (bottom).

Well, Susan, this is a fine mess you are in.

{ MAIRA KALMAN

VARIOUS

Maira Kalman is an illustrator, author, and designer whose artwork is featured in a new edition of Strunk and White's The Elements of Style. *She has created many covers for* The New Yorker, *including the famous map of "Newyorkistan" (created with Rick Meyerowitz). Her 12 children's books include,* Max Makes a Million, Stay Up Late, Swami on Rye, *and* What Pete Ate. *She also has designed fabric for Isaac Mizrahi, accessories for Kate Spade, sets for the Mark Morris Dance Company, and with her late husband Tibor Kalman under the M&Co. label, clocks, umbrellas, and other accessories for the Museum of Modern Art. Her work is shown at the Julie Saul Gallery in Manhattan.*

Illustration and cover by Maira Kalman for *The Elements of Style.* Design: Peter Buchanan-Smith. Illustration: Kalman

At M&Co. in the 1990s, you were largely responsible, with your husband Tibor Kalman, for a collection of very quirky products that found a huge market and consumed a large amount of your time. How did the watches and clocks with skewed numbers and conceptual faces and the folded paper paperweights come about?

Tibor was the driving force. He had incredible momentum, a million ideas, and great pragmatism. The designers at M&Co. worked like crazy. And what did I do? I was half in the background, half in the clouds, and working with Tibor all the time. I mean *all the time.* We never stopped thinking about ideas and projects. The watches were just, "How would it be interesting to play with how people see time?" The paperweights were more "aha!" Tibor sketched his ideas on yellow legal pads. If he did not like something, he ripped the page off the pad, crumpled it up, and threw it on the floor. He looked around one day and said, "That's it." He had invented a paperweight. There were many styles (blueprint, music). After Tibor died, I created the Prozac paperweight, which was a list of all the antidepressants people took. I thought every therapist would want one.

Now you're doing more products on your own?
Now I have ideas, and I understand how difficult it is to realize something new. I designed a dog raincoat out of plastic bags for my dog. I took it to Kate Spade. They designed a real coat and that expanded into people raincoats and bags and journals. It brought a beautiful income for a few years. But I would never have done it on my own. I much prefer to go to someone with the production capabilities. But actually, apart from a random idea every once in a while, I don't drive myself to create new products.

M&Co. was eventually sold, and others started making the products. At that time, you more seriously turned to children's books and illustration. But even this seems somewhat entrepreneurial. What prompted the creative turn of events?
The books were a natural development. I had stopped writing, and it was time to begin again. Of course, I had to find a publisher and then an agent. But this business of making books is a grand one.

So many of your projects come from such a fresh, unfettered, and noncommercial place. Yet they have legs in the marketplace. *The Elements of Style* book is not necessarily something one would think could have commercial success, but it certainly has cultural props. How did this come about? When did you conceive the idea of an opera based on it? And is there more you're going to do with it?
The Elements of Style happened because I was in Cape Cod on vacation poking about a church rummage sale. I was by the sea, where my brain was getting extra oxygen. And the idea was obvious and immediate. It took a few years to convince the parties—the E.B. White estate, the publisher, and so on. But it was a great publishing success and I loved working on it with absolutely no one telling me what to do.

I then contacted Nico Muhly, who I have known for years. He is a fantastically wonderful composer. And we

worked together on what this small night of music would be. I wanted to perform it in an unconventional space, and luckily Paul Holdengraber of the New York Public Library agreed to let us have the main reading room. These things all seem obvious to me. But he was brave. After all, I said to him, "A bunch of my friends and I want to bang some cans in the library reading room. Okay?" It was a spectacular night.

In the Maria Kalman universe, are there other entrepreneurial ventures that are on the boards waiting to be launched?
"The Principles of Uncertainty," which was an illustrated column for the *New York Times Select*, and now a book, will hopefully be an opera of some sort. But this takes time, and I am not sure what will happen. And I am thinking about making little movies and performance things. The point would be to get carried away with something interesting and fun that would come naturally.

How do you get your ideas?
I don't like to force ideas, just hope that they come. And I would like to have a little shop. Maybe in one of those stupendous metal coffee carts that sit on the corners in New York. I could see having a little business that I ran from there, with odd stuff and odd hours.

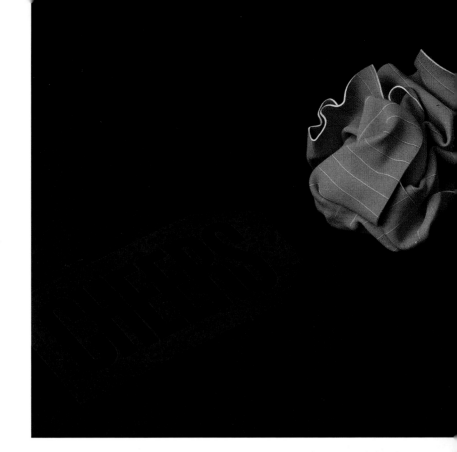

(Left and right) Crumpled
paper paperweights
where conceived
and designed with
Tibor Kalman at M&Co.

Doodle-covered rain hat,
one of many Kalman
fashions, produced and
illustrated by Kalman.

P22 Type foundry supports its continually expanding line of typefaces with an array of witty promotion pieces like this homage to the dollar Design: Richard Kegler.

All the font sets like this Art Nouveau collection, including "Arts and Crafts" and "Dard Hunter" fonts, are packaged with special flair. Design Kegler.

{ RICHARD KEGLER

P22 TYPE FOUNDRY

Richard Kegler, founder of P22 Type Foundry in Buffalo, New York, is interested in the history of art and design. He has been involved in various aspects of the book arts, from hand binding and hand printing to hypertext. P22's collection of fonts is a meeting of historical letterforms and the new processes of art and design.

How, when, and why did you start P22?
P22 (not specifically P22 Type Foundry) started in the late 1980s as a catchall for various projects where the name of a mysterious entity was preferred to having any one-person name attached. Why Buffalo? It has a unique combination of being very affordable and having a long history of the avant-garde with The Albright Knox Gallery and the University of Buffalo. My first studio was a sublet in the original Hallwalls space, which was started by Robert Longo and Cindy Sherman.

What does P22 signify?
The combination has no specific intended meaning. A rubber stamp was found with P22 on it in a plain sans serif face, and it became the de facto title for any art/mischief-related projects in college and after college.

You began by creating a font based on Duchamp's handwriting—a very novel approach to typography. How and why did you decide to resurrect all the passé styles that you've done so well?
Duchamp was made specifically as a somewhat minor detail in a large installation on Marcel Duchamp that was my master's thesis project. The marketing of the font and the subsequent artist-inspired fonts were a case of being in the right place at the right time.

Some would argue that you are perpetuating pastiche. Is there anything wrong with this?
I can't imagine that we are single-handedly perpetuating

pastiche. We certainly make it easier in some cases. With all of our fonts, we include full attribution to the historical source, which I think gets lost with other "revivals." I see current "designers" claiming credit for a design that is simply a digitization of a typeface. They don't acknowledge the source, and I think this is damaging to context. It's good to know the past and reference it when needed, but the jury may be out on revival. I think there are still more amazing designs from the past that are lost to time.

Let's talk about the business. Do you have a particular model or strategy that you follow?
The "business" really started off somewhat tongue-in-cheek. Our first business plan was written four years after we started in order to get a bank loan. The "plan" was basically describing what we had done in the previous four years. The deciding factor is often, "Do I like the idea?" If so, perhaps someone else will. Often my wife brings it back to earth by saying that my idea is stupid or great—sometimes simultaneously.

You sell fonts and products such as records, ties, books, and so on through gift and museum stores. Was this a hard venue to break into?
Breaking into it was easy. The first fonts were received with great enthusiasm from museum gift shop buyers. Since the dot-com crash of 2001, that market has become tougher and tougher. We have officially discontinued our packaged fonts and stick with font downloads off our website.

You are also commissioned to do fonts for particular cultural events such as exhibitions. How did this come about?

This was an extension of the museum gift shop offerings. Museums would have upcoming exhibits and wanted something a bit more interesting than coffee mugs, T-shirts, pencils, and so on. The Cezanne font, came to be a product for the Philadelphia Museum blockbuster Cezanne show. One product they developed actually used the Duchamp font because the Cezanne font had not yet been made.

What are your two biggest successes and why?

Cezanne has become our most widely known and widely used—and therefore widely pirated—font. Before Cezanne, our biggest seller was Hieroglyphic, which is simple ancient Egyptian hieroglyphics. We were picked up by the Book of the Month Club and Discovery Channel catalogs, and the exposure to a general audience just coming to terms with the desktop publishing revolution was amazing.

So, what were your two biggest failures?

Most of our projects are approached with a "break-even-quick scheme" mindset, our own Hippocratic oath: first, do no fiscal damage. For fonts, the biggest investment is time. Overhead has been relatively low for us, but to answer your question, the Futurismo soundtrack was not a big financial hit, but artistically I think it is one of the best things we have done.

Some of your fonts seem to be in the public domain, or you tweak them enough so you are not overtly violating copyrights. But others have estates attached to them. How do you handle these legal issues?

If we think something is public domain, we check to be sure. If it is not, we do everything possible to determine the proper rights holder and work out some agreement with the estate or foundation. We have not released

quite a few things that would be really great, but either due to no response or a negative response, we never went any further. We really try not to tweak. The Duchamp font was fuzzy. and ironically, our homage to the master of appropriation can no longer be sold.

Do you think you could have a business if not for the Internet?

No, absolutely not.

Package design for Daddy-O font set and ancillary materials. Design: P22 Type Foundry.

Package and souvenir mug for the Constructivist Font set designed in 1920s period style. Design: P22 Type Foundry.

A promotional tie accompanies the Insectile Font Set. Design: P22 Type Foundry.

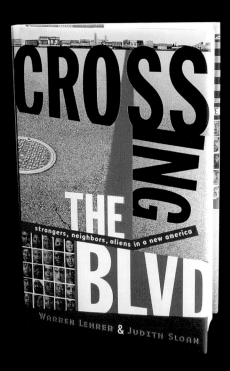

(Left) Cover for *Crossing the BLVD* by Warren Lehrer and Judith Sloan; design and photography: Lehrer, and (below) Crossing the BLVD exhibition installation. Story booth designed in collaboration with dotsperinch as part of the traveling exhibition.

{ WARREN LEHRER

EARSAY PUBLICATIONS

W*arren Lehrer, who founded EarSay with his wife, the performance artist Judith Sloan, is a designer, typographer, and author whose exhibitions and books, including* Crossing the BLVD, *explore the relationships between social structures and the individual. Lehrer teaches at Purchase College, SUNY, and the MFA Design program at the School of Visual Arts.*

You are a typographer, author, and performance artist. What made you start EarSay and what does it signify?

I started EarSay twice. Originally in 1983 as a small press, then in 1999, my wife Judith Sloan and I used the name again for our nonprofit, artist-based organization. EarSay is a made-up conjunction that connotes going out into the world with an open ear and collecting stories and voices, then channeling those voices and stories through my (our) creative process and coming out the other end with books, performances, radio, and audio works. EarSay also references synaesthesia. Although it sounds like a disease, synaesthesia is really a natural union of two or more senses that can result in seeing voices, hearing colors, tasting words, feeling the texture of numbers, and so on. We are all born with this fluid interrelation of senses (hence, ear, nose, and throat doctors).

Your books are more than paper and board. How do you think of them?

Back in the early 1980s, my books functioned both as scores for performances and as books that were meant to be read quietly alone. At that time, most literature was still written very much for the page. My own writing has always been very oral, very performable, so I tried to make books that used typography as a means of graphically translating vocal expression. I developed a system of notation that allowed for as many as 16 voices to be read on a single page, each voice represented through a different typeface and configuration. Eventually, I became interested not only in what characters were saying, but in what they were thinking. I worked to discover the shape of thought and capture it on the page.

Your *Crossing the BLVD* project is a pretty good example of working in cross-platforms.

Crossing the BLVD: Strangers, Neighbors, Aliens in a New America is a large documentary project portraying new immigrants and refugees in Queens, New York. In this multibranched project, Judith and I approached the book, radio documentaries, audio CD, traveling exhibition, mobile story booth, website, and performance in very different ways. The radio documentaries each focused on one story and conformed to certain protocols within public radio docs, whereas the audio CD gave us the freedom to create audio pieces and text music based on many of the same recordings made "in the field."

Do you self-finance your books or find publishers?

In the beginning, I did self-finance. I applied for and got some state and city arts grants, but it has been more worth my while to seek funding from private foundations. Receiving generous grants and fellowships from the Rockefeller Foundation, The Ford Foundation, the Greenwall Foundation, the Puffin Foundation, and other foundations allowed us to pursue projects that are large in scope and not inherently commercial. And yet, amazingly, recent political pressure on *private* foundations has caused some of them to curtail certain programs, outsource their funding mechanisms, and move to an "invitational" instead of an open application process. In other words, the days of the peer review panel are waning even within foundations, and a true elitism is on the rise.

Has elitism hindered your work?

In my own case, the very recent difficulty finding "subsidized" support for my work coincides with more interest from the commercial marketplace. I attribute this change to two things: one, the culture, for better and for worse, has become more "visual," and with the help of electronic media and the Internet, people are more accustomed to "reading" polyphonic, hypertextual formats. So, the world catching up to, or descending into, an aesthetic that is closer to one I've been working in for decades gives my work new currency. Two, my work has evolved in such a way that I'm much more concerned about the stories I'm telling and making sure that the means I use to tell them are effective. I learn from watching how people read my books or react in a theatre or interact with something meant to be interactive.

How much control do you maintain?

Even working with commercial publishers, I maintain near total control. I design and write (or cowrite) everything, then secure a publisher and deliver the book to the printer as a digital file. The cover designs are more open to editorial back and forth with publishers, but that has so far been for the best. The one thing I've really had to compromise on since I've not been the publisher is the paper. When I was publisher or copublisher, I would spare no expense on the paper. And when I sent books to individuals and even stores, the packaging was done with TLC. When we sent out the *French Fries* book, we wrapped it in printed waste sheets and enclosed a blue plastic fork and knife and a packet of ketchup into the custom-made corrugated box. I felt like I was sending out gifts to people. When someone else publishes, you lose that kind of touch. But you also lose having to stand on long, slow-moving lines at UPS and dealing with returns, and all of that, which I don't miss one bit. While I may "lose" some control by not doing everything myself, I have gained by working with really good editors and marketing people and through collaborating with information architects, musicians, sound engineers, actors, lighting designers, museum curators, and installers.

The Poetry Roll, a spread from *The Rise and Fall of Bleu Mobley*, an illustrated novel about the fictional author/designer of 101 books, written and designed by Lehrer.

Cover and spread for *French Fries*, an 1984 (before computer) experimental typographic concoction by Lehrer and Dennis Bernstein; designed by Lehrer.

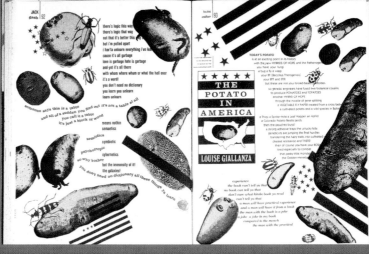

{ CHERYL LEWIN

BOW WOW BANDANAS

Cheryl Lewin ran her own design firm, Lewin Design Associates, in New York for 15 years and worked with clients such as Tiffany & Co, Brunshwig & Fils, and Disney Consumer Products. She then ventured into corporate life as vice president and creative services worldwide for Estée Lauder, vice president and creative director for Bloomingdale's By Mail, and brand creative director at Harry & David.

You started in graphic design and at the height of your success ventured into other areas such as a wallpaper collection, tabletop products, and fabrics. What prompted this, and what in your background do you think prepared you for it?

People have asked me, "Why did you choose design?" to which I reply, "I didn't. Design chose me." My love of graphic design has always included pattern and color. I grew up around aesthetically sensitive people. My mother was a photographer with amazing taste, and her husband was an architect. My eye for color, scale, texture, and pattern manifested in many ways from an early age. I found satisfaction in creating order in everyday life. I have always had a holistic approach to design—seeing the big picture and overriding theme in addition to details. Having run my own design firm in Manhattan, I was no stranger to running a business. I also learned a lot from my clients in terms of what it took to bring all the pieces together and develop, manufacture, and market a product.

What inspired you to start Bow Wow Bandanas?

I stopped to pick up a stray dog one country weekend morning. The pet industry was just in the beginning stages of evolving into what it is today. There were no options for a fashion-conscious hound like mine. I realized that the category of dog bandana could be elevated to another level. It was such an obvious idea. I realized that if I didn't do it then, someone else would. My entrepreneurial spirit kicked in and Bow Wow Bandanas was born.

(Left) Cheryl Lewin with her fashion-conscious hound Sally, the inspiration for the Bow Wow line.

Not only did you design the line, you started a business, and became the main retailer for the product. What did you have to learn in order to enter this competitive field?

There's nothing as powerful as a big idea and passion to get the juices flowing. I put together some prototypes and hired a car and driver for the day. I adorned my dog, Sally, with a Bow Wow Bandana, and we set out to take Manhattan. The driver stopped at every retail pet boutique in town. We would hop out and introduce our product. Sally was the best spokesperson/model, and the retailers seemed to really get it.

What, if anything, is the connection between this business and your graphic design business? What are the differences?

The big surprise was that I now wore the vendor hat, which was 180 degrees from the respect I got as a professional and senior member of a corporate landscape. We were now at the mercy of the retailers. In order to create a buzz, like any fashion collection, I committed a large part of our start-up budget to hiring a PR firm. We had a launch party and got some invaluable press. This was worth a lot when we displayed our laminated press coverage at our trade show booth that first year.

Canine models wearing two of the many variations of Bow Wow bandanas. Design: Lewin.

How successful have you been with Bow Wow Bandanas, and how do you keep it going?

We launched almost eight years ago and we are still in business. As with any fashion trend or new industry, the newness of it gave us a great bottom line the first few years. As the pet industry has matured, the novelty wore off as a lot more options entered the market. People no longer look puzzled when you speak of pet accessories. I was never in it just for the money. It was always a labor of love for animals and the fun of it. I keep my day job as a creative director and continue to fill orders on nights and weekends.

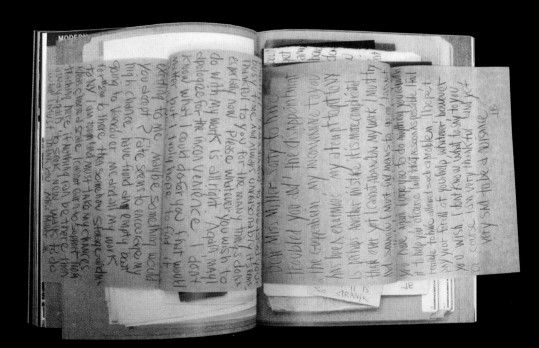

CONTENTS

Contents page and interior spreads from *Esopus*, which includes foldouts, diecuts, and all manner of special effects printing.

{ TOD LIPPY
ESOPUS MAGAZINE

T od Lippy, an editor, publisher and designer, was the founding editor of Scenario: The Magazine of Screenwriting Art *and cofounder of* publicsfear *magazine. Lippy has moderated panels at New York's American Museum of the Moving Image, the Austin Heart of Film Festival, the Independent Feature Project, and the New York/Avignon Film Festival. His 1999 short film,* Cookies, *was featured in over 20 film festivals. For the past three years, he has been the guiding force behind* Esopus, *a foundation-funded journal of art, design, culture, and the unusual.*

What is the goal of *Esopus*? And how have you gone about achieving that goal?

The goal of *Esopus* is to create an unmediated forum through which artists can reach the public directly with their work, with as little "filtering" as possible. I think I've been able to come close to achieving that goal by avoiding advertising, always communicating directly with contributors, and not hiring publicists or marketing people to promote the magazine.

The magazine is a total experience. Every medium but motion is tapped. What goes into your thinking behind the content? How, for instance, did you determine the features in the current (#8) issue?

I didn't want to create another art magazine or, for that matter, a film or literary magazine. I find that creative disciplines have become rather segregated (just go to the magazine section at a newsstand to get a very visceral sense of this) because of market pressures, and what ends up happening is that great contemporary art, more often than not, only gets to be seen and experienced by curators, critics, artists, and collectors and great foreign films are only seen by cinephiles in large urban environments. My thought was that if I made sure to keep the magazine resolutely cross-disciplinary, I would be able to pull in audiences from all of these different worlds and expose them to work from other mediums. This seems

to have worked, based on feedback I've gotten from subscribers. The only problem now is where it should go on the newsstand. I was at a Barnes & Noble not long ago and found it in the "Automotive" section!

What is the editorial process? The masthead shows advisors and aides, but do you generate the content by yourself?

I spend a lot of time looking at submissions and listening to tips I get from our board of advisors, our readers, past contributors, friends, and colleagues (not to mention interns). There's nothing better than getting a phone call or e-mail from someone I know and trust that starts with, "I just came across something that would be perfect for *Esopus.*" Generally, I either get a submission or solicit work from someone I admire. Then we get together to discuss what the possibilities are for their contribution. I'm happy to offer suggestions, but tend to be pretty hands-off if the person has a good sense of what they'd like to do. This works slightly differently for the CD, since the particular theme dictates what they'll be doing.

This is a "funded" magazine. How do you get and maintain the funding?

I knew when I came up with the idea of doing a magazine with no advertising (and with a heavily subsidized cover price), I would have to incorporate as a 501(c)(3) nonprofit

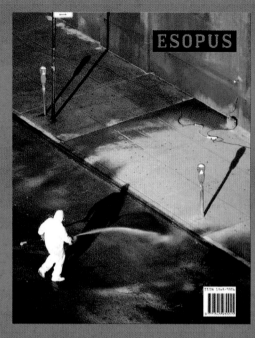

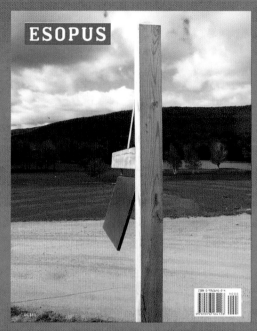

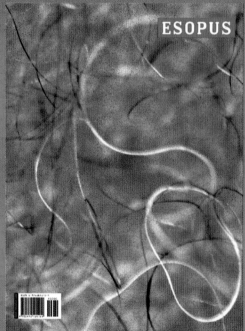

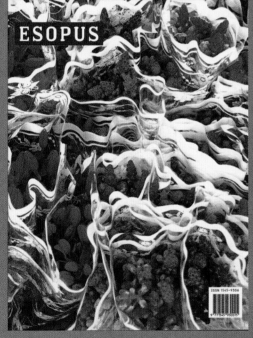

Esopus covers are never drawn, photographed, or designed to be commercial, but for their unmitigated audacity they attract the eye. The magazine is packed with unusual yet literate visual and text features. Design: Lippy.

and replace advertising income with donations and grants. We've been very lucky and have gotten substantial funding in the past couple of years from private organizations like the Andy Warhol Foundation and public agencies like the NEA and NYSCA. We also have an extremely generous (and quite large) group of individual donors who continue to make this whole thing viable. Maintaining these sources of income means near-constant grant writing and constantly scrabbling around for new potential donators. But it beats having to deal with advertisers!

You were not trained as a typographer, and yet your typography is well suited to your content. Where did your expertise come from?

I really don't have any expertise! I spent a torturous couple of months when I was putting together the first issue trying to come up with one sans serif and one serif font to serve as the "house fonts" for the magazine. After a lot of looking around, I settled on Trade Gothic for the former and Zuzana Licko's "Filosofia" for the latter. Both are elegant, beautiful fonts, but they also maintain (at least to my eye) wonderful neutrality. I've since come to also rely on a third one, Prestige, the classic typewriter font. I've ended up using one or the other of these for most article headlines, too (again, to keep things as neutral as possible), but occasionally I'll stray if the content seems to ask for it. An example would be the article we published on the history of the Ouija board and its use by artists, for which I used Captain Howdy, the font that appears on Ouija Boards.

I'd say that a lot of the *Esopus* design personality is rooted in "effects." You do foldouts, die-cuts, pop-ups, slip-ins, and all manner of other paper engineering. How do you decide what requires which approach?

With artists' projects, it's really up to each individual artist. The only limits on all of these projects are financial and logistical, but I try to be crafty about getting paper, specialty inks, and so on either donated or supplied at cost, and this has often made things possible that wouldn't have been otherwise.

You have established an Esopus foundation, and you put on performances pegged to each new issue of the magazine. What is your ultimate goal in all this entrepreneurial activity?

The mission of the Esopus Foundation is to create a forum where artists can reach the public directly with their work. I think everything we've done and will do in the future must keep that goal in mind. The events program is a great way to bring the magazine into three dimensions, and I hope to do more and more of these as time goes by.

Esopus is a visual feast, replete with fold-outs, tip-ins, gatefolds, diecuts, and multiple paper stocks, represented by this blueprint fold out. Design: Lippy

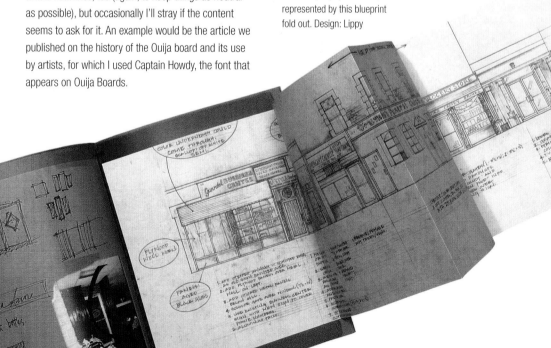

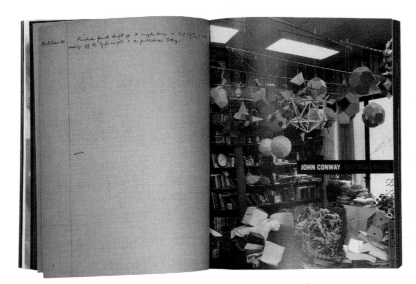

(Above) This cover is a photograph of a collection of illustrated notebooks featured in *Esopus*. (Left) John Conway is an artist featured in an expansive portfolio. Design: Lippy.

D.I.Y.

DESIGN IT YOURSELF

by
Ellen Lupton

BLOGS
BOOKS
BUSINESS CARDS
CDS
FLYERS
INVITATIONS
LOGOS
NEWSLETTERS
NOTECARDS
POSTERS
STATIONERY
T-SHIRTS
WEB SITES
WALL GRAPHICS
ZINES
AND MORE…

III A DESIGN HANDBOOK

Cover for DIY: *Design it Yourself* by Ellen
Lupton and the Graphic Design MFA
Program, Maryland Institute College of
Art. Cover photo: Nancy Froehlich.

{ ELLEN LUPTON

D.I.Y. DESIGN IT YOURSELF

*E*llen Lupton, a writer, curator, and graphic designer, is the chair of the Design Department at the Maryland Institute College of Art. She has also been curator of contemporary design at the Cooper-Hewitt National Design Museum since 1992 and has produced many exhibitions and numerous books, including Thinking with Type.

You are cornering the market with DIY design literature. What is your impetus in having students do this?

In most fields, graduate studies aim to produce new research that will enrich the knowledge of the field. Whereas undergraduate students focus on building their own personal skills and knowledge base, graduate students are supposed to generate an outward result. Publishing is an ideal vehicle for disseminating research. For graphic designers, the process of designing and producing publications is one of our primary areas of expertise and creative study. The graphic design MFA program at MICA has embraced publishing as both a creative medium and as a mode of sharing research. By working on publication projects, our students are learning how to create original content with real audiences in mind. They are learning about design, but also about how designed works become effective and viable in the real world.

Okay, why D.I.Y.?

A design revolution is currently underway in which ordinary citizens have increasing access to professional design tools and increasing interest in all aspects of design, from fonts to furniture. As professionals, we can put our heads in the sand and hope the amateurs will disappear or we can embrace this revolution and speak to the public about design thinking.

And why your book?

D.I.Y.: Design It Yourself was published by Princeton Architectural Press in 2006. To date, over 38,000 copies have sold. That's a healthy number for any book and it's evidence that people are interested in our message. We are now working on a more specialized book called *Indie Publishing: How to Design and Publish Your Own Content*. This book addresses anyone who wants to get involved in small-scale publishing. It demystifies the publishing process and emphasizes how good design can make a book stand out and function well for both its readers and its authors. The book is directed at artists, designers, writers, and anyone else who wants to get their own words and images out into the world.

The bigger message behind what we are doing is not D.I.Y. in particular, but design education in the broadest sense. We are creating educational tools to be used in various ways by various audiences. That's our contribution to the design discourse.

We've talked about the efficacy of DIY before, but what it really means is that in this day and age neophytes or indies can create their own cottage industries. Do you see more designers engaged in this practice?

D.I.Y. isn't just for "them," the amateurs; it's for "us," the professionals. The same revolution that is putting our tools and knowledge into the public realm is affecting our opportunities. Many designers want to develop products,

Spreads from *D.I.Y.*, on creating your own business card. All design by the Graphic Design MFA Program, Maryland Institute College of Art.

create tools, and publish ideas in addition to functioning according to the traditional B2B model of design practice.

What is the most difficult obstacle to overcome in the D.I.Y. business scheme?
People need to be clear about their own goals as D.I.Y. producers. For me, the business side is a means to an end, not the end in itself. I write books because I have a passion for producing knowledge that will have an audience; I have never made much money on the books, but the economics have been sufficient to support the process. If one's primary goal is to get rich, this is the wrong area of inquiry. Try hedge funds instead. But if your primary interest is in making ideas public, then the business side can be worked out to support the process in a satisfactory way.

How much business must a student or wannabe entrepreneur master in order to be successful?
I think that depends on how success is defined and what the goals are. Publishing is an established area with many protocols in place; it's not all that hard to get a book published if you are willing to put in the sweat. In contrast, introducing products such as toys, furniture, or flatware is much more complex from a production, marketing, and distribution point of view. Publishing is a fairly accessible area to get into.

As an educator, how much educating must you do to get students to become D.I.Y-ers?
At this point in time, having a D.I.Y. attitude is second nature to most students. They would much rather do something on their own (photography, video, illustration) than rely on professional services.

Do you think graphic design, and maybe design in general, is at something of a crossroads regarding the role of self-initiation versus client service?
I think client services will always dominate professional practice. It's much clearer economically, and there will always be a demand for design services. But I think we will see more designers pursuing independent projects.

Should designers be taught to serve the market or serve themselves?
Designers should serve the public. My students often talk about the "client" as the distinguishing feature of the design process. Designers are different from artists, the argument goes, because designers have clients. In actuality, what the client and the designer both share is a public. The client needs to get a message to a public, and without that audience, there is no reason for the client and the designer to work together at all. Reaching the public is the real goal of what we do; the "market" is a means to that end.

From book to *DIY* exhibition, entrepreneurism means exploiting all venues.
Photo: Froehlich.

{ ROSS MACDONALD

BRIGHTWORK PRESS

Ross MacDonald is an illustrator, writer, prop maker, and designer who founded
Brightwork Press. He is also a consultant on historic and period printing, paper,
and documents. Ross lives and works in Connecticut where he has an extensive
collection of nineteenth-century type and printing equipment.

(Left) MacDonald produced
Stupid Design for the back-
page of the *Virginia Quarterly
Review*, Spring 2006 issue
and (above) this cover
Illustration for the *New York
Times Book Review*.

**I can't think of a more entrepreneurial venture than
a small-press, old-type business. How did you, an
illustrator, get yourself involved with this obsessive
avocation?**

Actually, I started out as a printer and would occasionally
do small illustration jobs for pieces I was printing. In 1973,
I was lucky enough to get work at Coach House Press in
Toronto, which was an incredible education. A little later,
I started a small-press/letterpress shop, and by the early
1980s, I had phased out printing and was illustrating full-
time. But in the 1990s, I began self-publishing posters,
broadsides, and calendars. The process of working
with outside designers and printers inspired me to get
a small press and a few fonts of type. Long story short,
something snapped, and now I have a huge pile of type
and equipment.

**In addition to printing for yourself and others, you
use your metal type sources for making movie
props. How did you get into this field?**

I was approached about working on the movie, *Baby's Day
Out*, back in 1993. They needed a faux-1930s children's
book that would be a big part of the film and one of my
illustration styles at that time had the right feel. Because
the book is so closely tied to the action, I had to work on
set for about five months. I learned a lot and met a lot of
people. Of course, I thought that would be my first and
last film gig; how many times do they need a book for a
movie? But a few years later, I started to get calls from
some of those people or people they had given my name

to. It just snowballed pretty quickly from there. Usually, I get a call about doing one small piece and then next thing I know, I've done five months worth of work and thousands of documents, maps, letters, and books.

How much of your work is involved with producing printing versus props?

Most of my printing and design work these days is for movie props. It's pretty hard to get paid enough for the time involved in designing, hand setting, and hand printing. I think if I had spent more time (or any time, for that matter) pursuing ad agencies, or some of the other high-end clients for letterpress work, that I would have more pure printing work. It is incredibly hard to make a good living as a letterpress printer.

What has been the most ambitious entrepreneurial work you've done to date and why?

Setting up the press was a ton of work, but getting into the movie prop business was probably the most monumental. I had to spend a lot of time researching and educating myself on a lot of topics relating to period design, printing, paper, writing, and so on. A lot of the job involves being able to tell the director what something would have looked like, what kind of pencils they used in the eighteenth century, would a letter from 1860 have a stamp on it? An envelope? Would that typeface have been used at that time? When did they stop using the long *s*? Also, I had to teach myself how to do leather bindings, gilding, gold stamping, distressing, and leather tooling. And I also had to purchase a lot of things so that I would have anything I needed on hand for a quick job, such as acres of binding leather in every color, hundreds of sheets of dozens of different kinds of printing and specialty paper, inks and dyes, metal findings, gold for stamping, and other raw materials, as well as tools including binding tools, embossing stamps, and so on. I have five manual typewriters for making documents, old check writing machines, hundreds of rubber stamps, a dozen numbering machines, hot stampers, industrial hot plates, seal stampers, eight or ten punches, six or eight staple binders, and more.

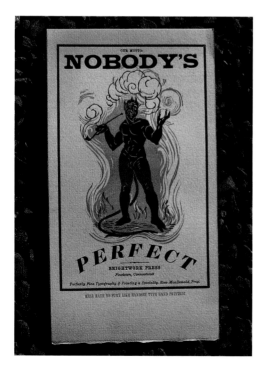

As a maven for type, what keeps you challenged?
The search for old lead and wood type, especially
interesting type, is always fun and very challenging. But as
someone who has spent a lot of time immersed in period
paper and who has several tons of period type, the biggest
challenge is to be able to design something that uses that
in a new and interesting way. It's easy to do something
that looks perfect for a certain period, but a lot harder to
take the same raw material and use it in a new way. And
of course, there's always the challenge of working with
old type.

**Do you see a day when this business will outweigh
all others?**
Right now, I'm really enjoying the mix. The ability to jump
from one thing to another and to combine them keeps
each individual one feeling fresh and interesting. But I'm
also toying with the idea of producing books. I doubt it'll
make enough money to become a full time thing, but you
never know. I never thought I'd be working half of every
year in the movie business, so I can't rule anything out.

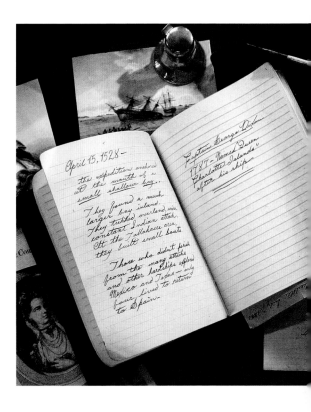

(Opposite page) MacDonald
makes letterpress cards at
his Brightworth Press.

(This page) He also produces
(as a sideline) props for
movies. Here are some for
*National Treasure: Book of
Secrets.* Nicholas Cage's
character's ancestor is
mulling over these papers
in a tavern when he is
approached by John Wilkes
Booth. The notebooks are
filled with references to
anything "Charlotte"—ships,
queens, islands, cities, etc.,
and stuffed with engravings,
maps, gravestone rubbings,
ciphers, letters, and other
documents.

{ JEFFREY METZNER
STICK

*J**effrey Metzner was a successful advertising art director and commercial producer before he devoted himself almost entirely to teaching at the School of Visual Arts. He teaches motion video unencumbered by commercial constraints. His book, STICK, featuring famous paintings, historical icons, and memorable events all rendered as stick figures, has blossomed into a business of cards, clothing, and calendars.***

You've been an art director and commercial director, so what inspired you to come up with these amazing stick figures?

The true story is that I was goofing on my then 8-year-old grandson. I was sitting on the front porch of my house in the country, and my grandson was on my lap.

"Gramps, did you know that I'm studying art history in school and I like it a lot...and I'm good at it!" he said proudly.

"Oh yeah, well hold on a minute, kid," I said, as I stood up to go inside to grab a pencil and a pad.

This is the interesting moment for me because I can draw, but instead of making a drawing, I made a stick figure drawing of a famous painting. When I finished it, I showed it to him warily and said, "OK wise guy, what's this?"

"Gramps, that's too easy," he said with a big smile. "It's the *Mona Lisa*."

"OK, and what about this one?" I asked, as I quickly did another stick drawing to show him.

"I don't know what the painting is called, but that's the same guy who made the *Mona Lisa*. He's got the same name as one of the 'Turtles' (He meant the *Teenage Mutant Ninja Turtles*.)

"Do you mean Leonardo?" I ask.

"Yeah, that's him."

I kept at it with him. He made one for me. We were laughing a lot when my son (his father) came out to the porch to see what was so funny. He did a stick drawing

GREAT MOMENTS IN ART

NOTE CARDS

Once Jeffrey Metzner came up with the idea, it stuck onto many products. Here *STICK Great Moments in Art* set of Notecards. Design: Metzner.

of *Scream*. We all cracked up. I stayed up late that night making more and more stick versions of great art. Soon my stick drawings lost their "stickiness." My "artistic" abilities activated. I went to my computer to help to keep the drawings naive and minimal. I learned a lot, reducing these great masterpieces down to their bare bones. And with most of history and children's illustrated stories I was free to invent the way the event looked.

So many books of this kind, conceptual gift books, find their way almost directly to the remainder pile. How did you insure its longevity?
There is no way to insure longevity. One thing that I did do was invest in a website. I did everything I could to get STICK-stuff to go viral. A friend of mine helped me make my fun website, www.STICK-stuff.com. The day Dailycandy.com included it in their blog we got 10,000 hits. I also have games, fun animations, and a link to the Random House website where one can purchase the STICK book.

Did you initially have other products in mind, beyond the scope of the book?
At the same time that I made a dummy of the book, I also made a 20-page dummy of STICK-stuff ideas. I had never had any experience with licensing before and that whole crazy world opened up.

How has the making and marketing of this consumed you?
This project has taken a lot of my time. I'd probably want $500,000 for the effort that I've made on my own behalf over the past two years. The truth is that a publishing company put books out into the world twice a year. Some of them make it, but 85 percent of them don't.

(Top) Metzner proudly sporting his *STICK* baseball cap.
(Above) And what started it all the *STICK* book. Design: Metzner.

Still from "One Hundred Minutes" video by Dragan Mileusnic

{ DRAGAN MILEUSNIC & ZELJKO SERDAREVIC

POTSCRIPTUM PUBLISHING

D*ragan Mileusnic and Zeljko Serdarevic formed a creative partnership in 2003 in Zagreb, Croatia, and together have created award-winning websites, edited and published a bestselling monograph on former Yugoslavia, and designed visual identities, and books. The work combines graphic design, fine art, and video.*

What were your initial forays into being an entrepreneur?

Initially, it was about having more control over the publications we create and not having to compromise with publishers over decisions we make as designers and editors. Also, working for corporations always left us feeling cheated by the disproportion of their profit to that of the authors. We love the idea of artists selling their music directly on the Internet; establishing Postscriptum publishing had a lot to do with that kind of ethic.

Let's talk about your entrepreneurial projects. What's your favorite and why?

Lexicon of Yu Mythology was the first book we produced together and it remains our favorite and most ambitious project. Because it deals with a subject that was taboo at the time (the memory of a federation torn apart by war only a decade before), numerous publishing houses had turned it down, so we had no alternative but to publish it ourselves. The fact that we created a bestseller came as a big surprise to us. It also convinced us we should keep on taking such risks in the future.

How did *Lexicon of Yu Mythology* come about?

Lexicon was initiated by a group of Yugoslav expatriates as an Internet-wiki in the late 1990s. Together with Rende, a small publisher from Serbia, we edited this material into a large volume encapsulating 50 years of cultural history shared in the former socialist federation. The publication had a profound cultural and political impact. A review aired by the BBC World Service in 2004 claimed that it was more beneficial in establishing postwar dialogue between Croatia and Serbia than "five years of combined efforts of all the politicians in the region."*

You work in various media. How did you accomplish the video for *Break, Blow, Burn*?

Our involvements with motion pictures for stage productions made us consider creating short films to make our book promotions more effective. For the Croatian edition of Camille Paglia's *Break, Blow, Burn*, we recorded readings of poems, giving each video an individual treatment informed by Paglia's interpretation. Our favorite part is Nadja Perisic-Nola's emotionally charged reading of Sylvia Plath's "Daddy," which we overlaid with text set in Fraktur after finding out that black letter shapes prevented Plath from learning her father's language. She once wrote that, "the very sight of those dense, black, barbed-wire letters" would force her mind shut like a clam each time she opened a German book.**

What were the challenges involved in Matrice Helvetice?

We were recently asked to organize a discussion on typography that would provide local context for the screening of Hustwit's "Helvetica" at the Croatian designers conference. We turned this down and did a short documentary entitled *Matrice Helvetice* (1924) with modernist icon Ivan Picelj instead. There seems to be a great need for some sort of overview of our design history (fragmented by wars and constant changes of political

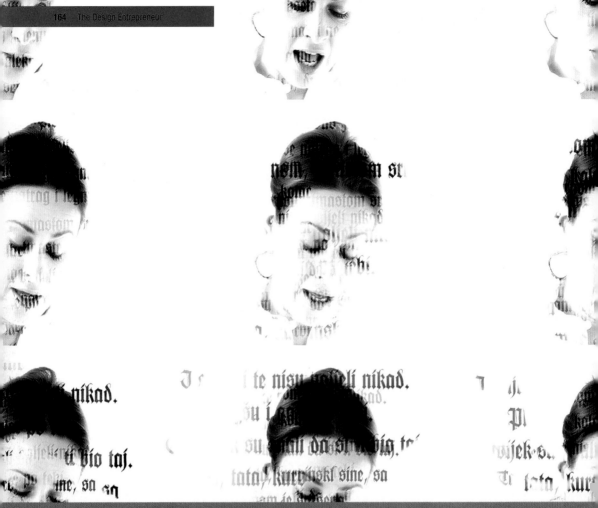

Stills from video promoting
the Croation edition of Camille
Paglia's *Break, Blow, Burn*.
Performer: Nadja Perisic-Nola;
video: Mileusnic.

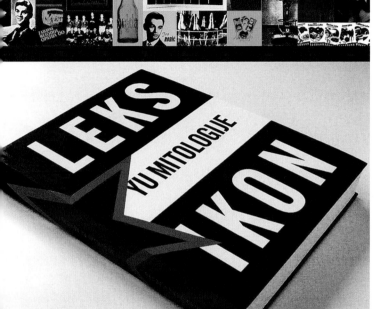

(Left) Multiple mediums come into play in this entrepreneurial effort. Here the video and book *Lexicon of yu mythology* is sampled. (Below) The pair also produced the Croation edition of Camille Paglia's *Break, Blow, Burn.* Design: Mileusnic and Serdarevic.

and economic systems), so we are now extending this successful project to a video series documenting various aspects of Yugoslav design history. Our intention is to establish a sense of continuity with this amazing period.

What's your most successful project and how do you measure success?

Although we experienced a more mainstream type of success as book publishers, we feel the movies we created "by the way" while working as video designers on international stage productions to be our biggest accomplishment. The essence of theater is elusive matter that's difficult to transfer to any media, but we believe our video recordings of *One Hundred Minutes* and *Inferno* do justice to the original performances. It is very rewarding to know we have managed to preserve many beautiful, fleeting moments that would have otherwise been lost.

What is your process for coming up with entrepreneurial ideas?

Before our careers as designers we were both involved in the fine arts, so self-initiated projects come to us naturally. But it is the designer's perspective, something we acquired working on commissioned projects, which helps us not to slip from "self-initiated" to "self-preoccupied." The designer's perspective also helps us see the potential of a stage production to become a movie that can become a book or a website (and vice versa). This is the typical mechanism behind all our entrepreneurial enterprises.

* This flattering statement is taken from a review by Snezana Curcic, aired by the BBC World Service on August 6, 2004.

** Camille Paglia quotes this from Sylvia Plath's autobiographical novel *The Bell Jar.*

{ JET MOUS

JET MOUS CERAMICS

Jet Mous is a Dutch ceramist/designer who was educated at the Academy of Arts in Ameersfoort, Holland. For many years, she combined teaching ceramics with her own work as a designer. She has worked mainly with clay, but also other materials such as textile plastics and paper. Mous repurposes the shapes of manufactured plastic bottles most commonly seen in laundry detergents and fabric softeners to cast colorful clay vessels.

Where did you study design?
I studied at the Academy of Visual Arts in Amersfoort, Holland, where I did several glass and ceramic workshops. I recently worked at the European Ceramic Workcentre in Den Bosch, Holland.

How and when did you start your firm?
From about 1980, I worked as a teacher and made my own ceramic work, both half-time. Since 1995, I have been a full-time ceramist/designer.

The work that you do has both beauty and wit. What determines the kinds of pieces you put into production?
It mostly starts by drawing my ideas on paper. I develop new ideas by looking at and thinking about completed work. I love to work with forms like circles, rectangles, cones, mathematic forms. Playing with those is endless and for me always inspiring. After the 2-D drawing, I try them in 3-D in clay. If it suits me, I hope it suits my clients. I think it is hard to design things for clients in the first place as a one-person firm. When you work in a team and can explore the market, maybe you can design successful client-aimed products, but even then the great thing of working as an artist/designer is to follow your own ideas, instinct, curiosity, or whatever drives you. It is playing with material, exploring it, and forgetting about clients in the beginning.

How do you manage your entrepreneurial work?
I take a rational approach. If the production is very complicated, or risky, and therefore too expensive, I stop after making a few products. I always try to realize complicated forms because that teaches me a lot. And of course, if the product doesn't sell anymore, I stop producing it.

You do jewelry, tabletop accessories, and fashions. Are you trained in all, or did you teach yourself?
I got an education as an artist in many disciplines in a rather traditional way. I learned an awful lot about all kind of materials, which has been very useful. I choose to work in clay, offering the possibility to produce my own work. So I am trained in part, but I learn mostly from my failures.

Your work is so colorful. Is there an aesthetic philosophy behind your color palette?
I think my forms simply ask for plain, bright colors.

From drawing to porcelain the *Cow-and-Flower Vase* comes "ceramically" to life. Design: Jet Mous.

(Left and right) More ceramic marvels, including a bracelet from Mous' jewelry line, and a three-piece vase–each piece can be used separate or together in multiple ways. (Bottom) Colorful and modern, Mous' collection of ceramic vases are humorously reminiscent of detergent bottle forms and shapes. Design: Mous; photography: Jan Dekker

The great thing of working as an artist/ designer is to follow your own ideas, instinct, curiosity, or whatever drives you. It is playing with material, exploring it, and forgetting about clients in the beginning.

How well did your cow-and-flower lamp do in the marketplace?
My work sells rather well. My vessels, cylinder vases, and cleaning-bottle vases are successful. Their photos appeared in many magazines all over the world. Since I have the website, I have contact with galleries and art shops in different countries. The cow and flower vases are new and I haven't done much to promote them. I've sold a few in London and they will be on display at a great fashion event in Amsterdam in July.

Do you test these things or let intuition rule?
I do not test them. I make a few, put photos on the website, or send emails to promote them, and if people order them, I can produce them rather fast (sometimes with a little help from my friends).

Would you call yourself an entrepreneur or a designer who creates original products?
I am a designer who is lucky to be able to sell the products I create.

Art Out of Time

UNKNOWN COMICS VISIONARIES, 1900–1969

DAN NADEL

{ DAN NADEL

PICTUREBOX

D an Nadel is a Brooklyn-based writer, editor, and proprietor of PictureBox, *which conceives and produces books on comics and illustration. His work has appeared in the* New York Times, Print, *and* Metropolis. *He is Assistant Professor of Illustration at Parsons School in New York. Nadel won an Emmy for the codesign of Wilco's* A Ghost is Born *CD package.*

You are not a trained designer, but you have become an art/design publisher, editor, writer, and educator. How'd you pull that off?

I've spent the better part of my life studying, talking about, and obsessing over visual culture. Now, that alone doesn't really give me any authority, but somehow I've always trusted my own taste. That might be sheer arrogance, but I feel like I have a very strong eye for visuals and a mind for how they function in both intellectual and physical spaces. I also think there is no substitute for a broad and deep understanding of visual culture history. That alone can make a decent art director into a really good one. On a more practical level, I pulled it off by constantly letting people teach me things. In college, I let bibliographies dictate my reading choices and now in life, I am surrounded by amazing artists, designers, typographers, historians, illustrators, cartoonists, and so on. Also, I'm ornery, restless, and have a lot of trouble with authority. That makes me look under rocks and around corners and breeds a constant dissatisfaction that pushes me on and helps me do all of those things.

Early in your untrained career you started a design/ publishing firm called PictureBox. Can you give me some details about how this came to be?

I started PictureBox with a partner, Peter Buchanan-Smith (see page 19), in 2002, with the intent to package and publish books. I wanted to try to make immersive, experiential visual books unlike anything else on the market. We codesigned and won a Grammy for the package design of Wilco's *A Ghost is Born* CD and codesigned and edited *The Wilco Book* together, among other projects. Peter left at the end of 2004, and I continued on. The idea is that PictureBox is a visual hub—a publishing house and a community, and a consultancy. It takes on all manner of projects guided by my gut feelings and tastes.

You are currently the sole proprietor of PictureBox, and you've found a unique and rather successful niche publishing books on comics and illustration. What did you do to make this work? Indeed, it's not cheap to both acquire rights and then publish. How much of this is your own investment?

I sell books—seriously. Acquiring the rights is not expensive, as most of the artists I work with understand the economics of this arrangement and are happy to trade that for complete creative control and someone they can trust. PictureBox exists to facilitate artists' visions—no nonsense. And I have a great accountant and lawyer who make everything transparent to my artists. A huge amount is dependent simply on the way I do business. I have some small business loans, but otherwise I sell books online, at tradeshows, art fairs, comic fairs, print fairs, and music festivals.

Your books are well designed and appropriately designed for the market and audience. How do you make this happen?

I am a very finicky and obsessive watcher of all things visual, and I have a lot of ideas for how I want things to be presented. I then work with designers I trust who have a like-minded sensibility. It's a good collaboration and it's mostly all about giving the designers as much leeway as possible. The designers I work with most—Circle and Square and Helene Silverman—are extremely smart and savvy designers who are interested in content and the best possible expression of the material their work is containing and enhancing. And we rarely ever disagree. So, the basic answer is that I work with people with whom I'm in sync and just let them go to town.

How do you go about developing your product line, if I may call it that? Do you test? Or do you simply publish what strikes your fancy? Or is there something in between?

It's a lot of instinct. I like working with people who are, well, good to work with. I don't test, but I also don't publish whatever I want. I look for books that I feel transcend their obvious categories. I like graphic novels that will appeal to art lovers or photography books that document an artistic culture or period. So, I'm looking for statement in print form that resonates beyond their initial reading. I'm also looking for content—everything I publish is communicating and not taking any shortcuts. It's about giving the audience something to chew on.

What do you foresee as the future of PictureBox? What are your long-term goals and will you remain totally involved in the print world?

The future is more books. I have a couple of historical design surveys planned and am beginning to publish Manga. I'm also working with some bands and a film director on books of their own. The future is more and better, to a point. I want to keep it small, but the books themselves are increasingly ambitious. My new website is launching soon, so that will widen the audience, I hope, and we'll go from there.

Nadel scours the alternative art scene to find comics artists to publish. These are a few of the original books conceived, produced, and published by PictureBox, Inc.: (Left) The cover for *CJB Da Dog*. Design: Ben Jones.

(Right) Spread from the Book Me A Mound. Design: Jesse Rymill; prehistoric ape family drawing: Trenton Doyle Hancock.

THE MOUND STORY BEGINS WITH AN AVERAGE PREHISTORIC APE FAMILY. THE FATHER'S NAME IS HOMERBUCTAS. HE IS MARRIED TO ALMACROYNA. TOGETHER THEY HAVE TWO APE CHILDREN : A SON, BROUTHESCAM, AND A DAUGHTER, CROMALYNA. HOMERBUCTAS HAS THE PHYSICAL FEATURES OF A TYPICAL PREHISTORIC APE-MAN (i.e, LOW-HANGING BROW, PROTRUDING MUZZLE MOUTH), BUT HE DIFFERS FUNDAMENTALLY FROM OTHER APE-MEN. YA SEE, HOMERBUCTAS HAS A KNACK FOR TURNING IMPULSION INTO COMPULSION. HE HAS AN EYE FOR BEAUTY, BUT KNOWS NO MODERATION. HIS DESIRE TO BE SATIATED IN THE PRESENCE OF BEAUTY ULTIMATELY CREATES A RIFT BETWEEN HIMSELF AND HIS APE FAMILY.

AND SO IT BEGINS ....

{ GARY PANTER

THE MAN CAT TOY

*G*ary Panter, the "King of the Ratty Line," is a comic strip artist, underground *cartoonist, and Internet animator who is also a three-time Emmy winner for his production design on* Pee-Wee's Playhouse. *He is the creator of* Jimbo, *a post-nuclear, punk rock cartoon character whose adventures were chronicled as a comic strip in* RAW *magazine. Panter is the recipient of the 2000 Chrysler Design Award.*

You have been making comics, shadow puppet performances, toys, and all manner of other creative stuff in an entrepreneurial way for many years. Do you consider yourself an entrepreneur?
Unless one is rich or incredibly lucky, surviving as an artist requires a certain amount of entrepreneurial thought. I do like making models, or miniatures, of stores, bands, publications, theaters, houses, and so on. Many years ago, I wrote a satirical, pro-capitalist manifesto, "The Rozz Tox Manifesto," in which I encouraged artists to compete in the entertainment marketplace.

Let's talk about some of the recent products to emerge from your twisted mind. How did "The Man Cat Toy" come into being?
I was working with some friends on a small puppet project and was doing a lot of clay modeling, plaster casting, and latex pouring. The Man Toy was a test. When one of my cats became obsessed with it, I decided to market it.

Is this intended for mass production or is it one of your "art" pieces?
The Man Cat Toy is an art project that falls within the larger project, the online Gary store, which Helene Silverman and I run on my website. Though I sold a few cat toys, the function of it is more as content for the shop. If the shop has no content or entertainment aspect, people

won't stay there or send their friends. So the shop is an art project wherein objects are for sale, though not all are expected to sell. And it needs to be like a magazine with stories to tell.

How do you distribute this and the decidedly perverse Cicada rubber toy, which on the back says, "Made from latex rubber and real cicada shells from Panter's yard"?
Only at the online shop. I hope they don't sell. The shells are from my yard in Brooklyn or my parents' yard in East Texas. The price is high to discourage sales and promote outrage.

All these toys have great labels and tags. What's more challenging for you—the toy concept or the branding?
These things are easy to conceive, but very time intensive in that they involve linoleum block cutting, printing, stapling, latex pouring, cicada shell collecting, or cat watching.

You also designed a coaster. Why?
I like having all the categories of merchandise addressed in the shop, just like in a real department store. The online shop attracted the attention of an industrial designer, Paul Lacotta, who wanted to collaborate. I gave him shredded

---

Woven patches of some of Gary Panter's quirky comics characters.

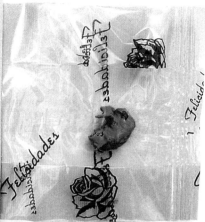

(Top and middle) The Cicada Rubber Toy made from shells in Panter's yard in Brooklyn or his parent's yard in east Texas.

(Bottom) The Man Cat Toy, a latex rubber man produced for fun. All toys sold through the online Gary Store, garypanter.com.

drawings and documents from my paper shredder and
he invented the coaster. He is working on generation
two coaster now.

**It makes perfect sense that you would design
patches because Jimbo and your other characters
are so emblematic. But talk about how you package
these and how you sell them?**
I want the online store to be a personal, aesthetic
experience for the customer, so I hand-pack the items.
The small items I posit in cereal boxes that normally would
get thrown away. The packaging is colorful and a good
background for the items—the juxtapositions are funny.

**Speaking of sales, how successful, in a monetary
way, have these products been for you?**
The return has been worth it. We are not getting rich
from it, but some money is made and a lot of nice people
are met in the process. Maybe they will buy paintings
someday.

What's next for Panter the entrepreneur?
My 1983 LP, *Pray For Smurph*, will be released on CD
from Overheat Records in Tokyo this year. I am designing a
freak flag to be included with the record. Once I explained
what a freak flag is (that there is no such thing) and its
origins in the Jimi Hendrix song "If 6 Was 9," my friends
at Overheat were very excited to help me make it.

(Top and middle) One-of-a-kind
plastic plates hand-drawn by
Panter. (Bottom) Plastic coaster
from an edition of twenty for the
Gary Shop. These coasters, sold in
sets of four, feature the shredded
reject marker drawings and legal
documents of Gary. Each set is
accompanied by a certificate
of authenticity signed and
numbered by the artist. Designed
and manufactured by Paul La Cotta

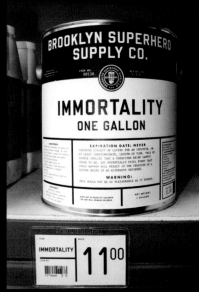

{ SAM POTTS

BROOKLYN SUPERHERO SUPPLY CO.

am Potts runs a generalist graphic design practice in New York City. He designed all the branding, packaging, posters, and store materials for the Brooklyn Superhero Supply Co. as well as the publications and website for the superhero store's alter ego, 826NYC, a nonprofit writing and tutoring center in Park Slope, Brooklyn.

How did you come to do all the very cool product designs for the Brooklyn Superhero Supply Co.?
The superhero store is the storefront for 826NYC, a nonprofit writing and tutoring center for students of all ages (see Dave Eggers interview on page 106). The center is completely free, and open to all, and offers after-school tutoring, workshops on a wide variety of topics (candy, novel writing, filmmaking, monsters and robots, cheese), school field trips in which classes write stories together, and a host of other such programs. It's also a place where young writers are published. We've published two anthologies of assorted writing, three full-fledged books, and countless booklets of work from specific workshops.

Who is the audience?
Primarily superheroes and sidekicks. I would have thought that's obvious, but you'd be surprised who comes in looking for a superhero "costume." We don't sell costumes; we do sell superhero uniforms. We don't cater to villains of any kind, but we do promise that villains who have a change of heart will be welcomed. We also have a fair number of civilians buying gifts; we assume these gifts are for superheroes. Who else could possibly need Gigantor gloves or the cross section of a giant worm?

What was your concept behind the products in the store? Was it tongue-in-cheek or were you playing it straight?
The design of the store and the products all flow pretty much from the idea of a hardware store for superheroes. The language of the labels is very retail sounding, emphasizing features and usefulness in affirmative tones, even in the case of FantastiCo's Pretty-Good Forcefield, which has "some of the properties of an actual force field," and which closely resembles a net. I've found in designing the labels that making the thing look serious is the right way to go, so there aren't any cartoon figures or muscle-bound mascots or anything that looks comic-bookish. Our generic store brand is just black and white and looks more than a little like a Campbell's Soup can. A straight face works best when dealing with the store customers as well. It's been really interesting to see how people react; at first, some are wary that a joke is being played on them and they want to know literally what's in a can of Muscle. But if we don't tell them and say something like we have no idea because it's made by yak farmers in Kamchatka, they kind of catch on and pretty soon they're totally playing along, explaining these very things to other customers. Which is so satisfying, to see it work like that.

An assortment of products designed and invented by Sam Potts for the Brooklyn Superhero Supply Co.

(Left) The Brooklyn Super Hero company is known for its odd commodities. *The Secret Identity Kit for One American Male* presents what has been called "A straight face on a joke product."

(Below) And another must-have, integral piece of Superhero Apparel: Hood Design: Potts

How important is design in your product conceptions?

The design is important to a degree and customers sometimes remark on the graphic design of the place, but I honestly don't think it's design in the graphic, visual sense that's making the place work. I mean, it's a superhero supply store—how could that *not* hook people? The humor is what's *really* working and that's in the way things are designed to the extent that the design presents a straight face on a joke product, as we talked about, but it's really in the conception of the products and the writing. A detail like the nutritional information in Antimatter (anticalories, antiprotein, etc.)—it's a small touch on the back of the label, but it's so satisfying that the concept is played all the way out like that. I think that's what works more than typefaces and "branding" and so forth.

Is there an overarching approval process, or is it anything you decide to do?

Not exactly anything I, Sam Potts, decide to do, but certainly I think that between Scott, myself, and some other key people, we're free to try anything that's funny "on message" (that is, useful to the superhero community) and will sell or enhance the store.

What's next?

We have several ideas for some new brands of products including invisible merchandise for our invisible customers and a line of impossibly large machines and gadgets, which I think exist in another dimension and are mostly rentals. I'm hoping some of the designers who've offered will come through with some designs for new brands or posters. Eventually, we hope to make our own licensed products. If you know anyone who can produce child-friendly, rubber grappling hooks, we really need a good supplier.

Hot Dog
BUN & KETCHUP
2
30
© 2003 TYPE 1 TOOLS LLC

Rice
1/2 CUP COOKED
1 1/2
22g

Peas
1/2 CUP COOKED
1
12g
© 2003 TYPE 1 TOOLS LLC.

Fish
ALL KINDS
NOT BATTERED
0
0g
© 2003 TYPE 1 TOOLS LLC.

(Above) FlashCards from Type1Tools a teaching aid for parents of and children with Type 1 diabetes. Design: Doug Powell

type1tools®

Helping families manage life with Diabetes

{ DOUG POWELL
TYPE1TOOLS

*D*oug Powell is a designer, business strategist, and principal of Schwartz Powell Design, a Minneapolis, Minnesota-based firm he founded with his wife, Lisa Schwartz, in 1989. The husband and wife team also founded HealthSimple, which brings creative solutions and better design to the disease management experience. In early 2007, McNeil Nutritionals, a division of Johnson & Johnson, acquired HealthSimple. Currently, Doug serves as HealthSimple brand creative director.

In addition to serving your clients you've created an entrepreneurial, design-based product, Type1Tools, a teaching aid for parents of and children with Type 1 diabetes. Did this start in a digital way or in a traditional way?

The development of the original line of Type1Tools products was very much rooted in our experience as print designers. All of the pieces in that line were print pieces. There were several reasons for this: first, and most importantly, this is what we knew how to do and this was where we had the most developed network of production resources; second, this allowed us to have complete creative control over the designs—so we weren't dependent on other creative professionals to develop the line; finally, we were able to get the products out to market very fast, again, without having to depend on others. The whole process happened within our professional comfort zone.

In order to communicate your wares, the Web has become very important. What did you have to learn about this platform to be effective?

Once the products were complete, we had to find the best, most effective, and most direct way to bring them to market. In 2004, Web-based e-commerce was just hitting its stride, and this was clearly the best option for our new business. The process of building this site was very much

out of our comfort zone, so we relied on the Minneapolis firm, IdeaPark, which was our primary Web development partner throughout the evolution of the sites.

Currently, we are collaborating with our key business partners to develop new products that will be delivered through the Web and other online technology. Truly, the most important skill I have in this area is finding the most skilled collaborators and working effectively with them.

Maya Powell using FlashCarbs, which feature colorful pictures and graphics to help children and adults learn the carb values for common foods—making it easier to choose foods wisely and make calculations at mealtime.

We have always worked with skilled collaborators, and we have become very good at determining when we need help and utilizing our network to find the right resources for our needs.

Because you've become so successful with this product, are you giving up many of your service-based clients?

In early 2007, McNeil Nutritionals, LLC, acquired HealthSimple. Selling our business was never a part of our original long-term planning for HealthSimple, and our initial connection with McNeil was a result of a very typical sales relationship. However, we quickly realized a great deal of synergy between our businesses and began discussing how we might work together in a more meaningful and sustainable way. The acquisition was the culmination of these discussions. We are thrilled to be working closely with an organization that can help us bring our products—and our design-driven approach to health education—to a much broader audience than we ever could have touched on our own.

Since the acquisition, Lisa and I have been retained by McNeil to serve as consultants as they build the HealthSimple brand. I am working as creative director for the HealthSimple brand.

What are the challenges that you were prepared and unprepared to deal with in this new entrepreneurial role?

We were completely unprepared to address the "hard-core" aspects of planning and building the original product line into a full business. By this, I mean we had to figure out how to handle things like writing a formal business plan, financial projections, intellectual property, product distribution, and many other pieces. This was akin to learning a new language after speaking only English your whole life.

But we have always worked with skilled collaborators, and we have become very good at determining when we need help and utilizing our network to find the right resources for our needs. That is exactly how we solved the problem of our lack of traditional business acumen.

As a design entrepreneur, how important, compared to your other concerns, is design?

For us, design and, more broadly, creative thinking has been the pivotal difference in our success. Beyond being the key instigator in our original product development, our ability to see the business world through the lens of design has given us a very unique perspective that has been a valuable point of distinction for us. We worked with many lawyers and MBAs during the development of our business, and while they provided much value to us, their perspective was very much tainted by their training and experience in these fields. This made it very hard for them to see our business with a fresh eye and recognize the unique value and potential it holds.

How do you see this changing your life?

For one, it has given Lisa and me a way to make a mid-career shift that allows us to use our experiences as designers in a way that is very different from how we were working previously. For both of us, this has been a refreshing and welcome career change.

(Right) A page from type1tools website Type1tools.com.

(Below) CarbWise Meal Worksheets are handy, pre-printed Post-It® Note forms that simplify the process of counting carb choices and calculating the proper insulin dosage at mealtimes.

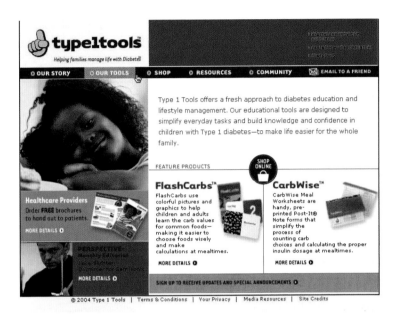

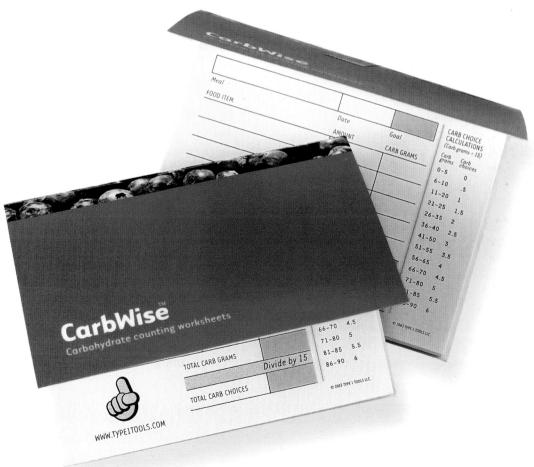

{ ROBYNNE RAYE

NOVELTY ITEMS FOR BLUE Q

R obynne Ray is a designer and cofounder of Modern Dog design studio in Seattle, Washington. The studio produces posters, logos, custom lettering, packages, products, and advertisements. Modern Dog's alternative music and culture posters chronicle the Seattle grunge scene.

Modern Dog in Seattle spend a lot of their time creating novelties for Blue Q. Their favorite is Patron Saint of Parking car air freshener.
Design: Robynne Raye, Modern Dog Design Co.

With a name like Modern Dog, what were you trying to say to the world, or at least to the clients you wanted to reach?

At the time Mike Strassburger and I started our company, the going trend for design companies was names that sounded like law firms. They all were named after their principals. Seattle examples included Hornall Anderson, Tim Girvin, Pat Hansen, and Art Chantry. We originally thought we should not make waves and just do what's appropriate, so we actually started as Raye Strassburger. Then we came up with the pseudonym of "Modern Dog" that we used to sign posters. Raye Strassburger felt so nauseating that we just dropped it after three months and went with Modern Dog as our name, which just felt natural to us. The ultimate message was that we are who we are and we are not going to do things just to fit in. We attracted clients who felt the same way. Our name acted as a filter. If someone was turned off by it, they probably would not like our work and we wouldn't be happy working with them either.

Let's talk about being an entrepreneur. Being a twenty-year-old business makes you entrepreneurs, but how much of your weekly or yearly routine is devoted to self-generated commercial or noncommercial products?

We create two to four posters a month for self-promotion. On average, the posters, take 10 hours to design. We don't sell the individual posters and typically the design fee goes toward the printing costs, but we do make money indirectly through job leads. In recent years, the posters have been predominantly music-related, but we also have a sizable theater poster portfolio because in the late 1980s through the mid 1990s we worked regularly for several local and national theaters. We ended up putting those posters on two decks of cards that have sold in museums and bookstores in Seattle as well as places outside of Seattle (Cooper Hewitt, Denver Art Museum, etc.). The first deck, created in 1995, sold out in four years, so we created a second deck with completely different posters in 2001. Our third deck is on hold because we don't want it to compete with our poster book that is due out in 2008. Besides the occasional Modern Dog T-shirt, all of our other products are distributed through Blue Q. Our fourteen-year relationship with Blue Q has enabled us to feel that the products sold under their label are as much ours as theirs.

You've done many "novelty" style products for Blue Q (which is also represented in this book) and you do earn royalties on successful wares. So how do you go about conceiving these items?
Yes, we do earn royalties, which really makes it worthwhile. Many times, Mitch Nash from Blue Q and my partner Mike will talk on the phone about new product ideas and brainstorm together. That can start with an idea Mitch has that he wants to run by Mike, or vice versa. Sometimes Mitch will call us and say he's thinking about adding a new type of product to his wares and will pay us to give him a giant, totally free-form list of ideas. When we do that, we really do not censor ourselves.

How much of your entrepreneurial conception is based on design versus idea? And where does the design come to play?
In regards to Blue Q, the ideas always come first, and design is just used to clarify and enhance the idea. If we ever feel like design is what makes the idea, then we know the idea is too weak to be commercially successful, and we make adjustments or just scratch it. Posters are totally different; they can be based completely on style, as the style can be the idea.

What are your favorite—or most successful—entrepreneurial activities?
The vacation part.

Ever consider founding Modern Dog Enterprises to package and brand your sense of humor?
We already do it through Blue Q, without all the manufacturing, production, and distribution headaches, and no financial risk.

What, after your milestone year, comes next?
Year 21.

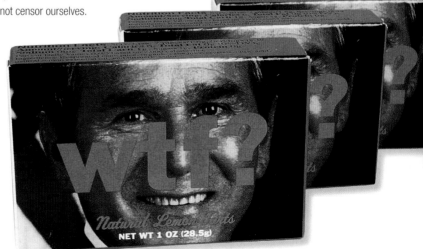

For wtf? (or what the. . .?) Raye borrows the familiar image of the U.S. commander -in-chief for a lemon tart package. Design: Raye, Modern Dog Design Co.

{ HANS DIETER REICHERT

BASELINE MAGAZINE

Hans Dieter Reichert is editor, art director, and publisher of Baseline, *the type and design magazine, based in Kent, England. He is also director of HRD Visual Communications whose clients include Phaidon Press, Norman Foster Architects, and the British Museum.*

What prompted you to publish *Baseline*, a magazine that was at one time owned by Letraset, the big press-down lettering company?
Letraset started the magazine back in 1979 as an A4 (traditional magazine size) publication in two colors. The magazine was mainly distributed via the Letraset outlets/ shops throughout the world. The contents of the first nine copies were mainly new typeface designs, type history, and type-related technological aspects. During the 1980s and early 1990s, these contents changed slightly and became more graphic design oriented. The visual appearance also changed—bigger format and printed in four colors—yet the visual presentation of the contents had no real concept and deteriorated.

In 1993, Letraset asked HDR Visual Communication to redesign the magazine with issues 17 and 18. Both magazines were immediately successful with Letraset and the design community, which resulted in winning several major international awards. In 1995, HDR approached Letraset with the aim to buy the magazine. We were quite enthusiastic about the publication, had so many good ideas, and wanted to develop the publication further. During that year, we founded a separate company, Bradbourne Publishing Ltd., in order to publish the magazine. In those first years, we learned how to become a publisher. It is a skill to create a publication, but it is another skill to distribute it internationally!

Baseline has been published from your design firm, HDR Design in Kent, England, for many years. How much of your overall time does the magazine take, and how much of your resources are devoted to it?
The production/publishing of *Baseline* is an integral part of HDR's work. Our design company is relatively small. Headed by myself, Veronika, approximately three or four designers, and a student. We work quite intensely on each issue (commissioning articles and art, editing, designing, and performing production work before it gets printed, bound, and distributed). Besides the magazine, we have also been working on other publications, corporate work, and electronic designs.

The magazine is beautiful. Is this a place where you can experiment with design? Or must you keep it fairly consistent to the content you are presenting?
The underlying structure is a 12-column grid, which gives the magazine an overall flexible structure to create each article individually. The inspiration for the designer is the contents of the article. We work from the inside to the outside—sometimes reflecting the contents or contrasting the contents. In any case, the designers for *Baseline* are editorial designers and are accepted by the authors. To us, the magazine is not just a carrier of information, it is a visual, tactile, and sensual object that reflects a complete holistic design approach and, hopefully, will be seen as a celebration of graphic design.

Pages from *Baseline* (top), and a scene from the HDR design studio in action (middle). HDR publishes, edits, and design this long-running typographic magazine.

On what type of business model do you run *Baseline*? You take some advertising, but how much of the magazine pays for itself?
The magazine is financed by a healthy international subscription base. We also have sales in commercial outlets and a bit of advertising (only four pages per issue). We believe that these select ads receive more recognition and appreciation from the readership than in magazines that are cluttered full of ads.

The magazine is a quarterly, but do you adhere to a strict schedule or does it play second fiddle to your design business?
We pay a lot of attention to details and we don't like to compromise on the production. If it comes out a month or so later than scheduled, it is usually due to late entries or print and finishing issues, since a certain aspect of the process is hand finishing (using white cotton gloves to avoid marking). It is important that the end product is produced to our satisfaction.

Foldout Poster from *Baseline* magazine and covers, which always feature details from elements shown in the magazines. Design: HDR Design.

Cover of Furore magazine, a popular culture journal with
emphasis on visual phenomena. Design: Piet Schreuders

{ PIET SCHREUDERS

DE WOLKENKRABBER, DE POEZENKRANT, FURORE

*P iet Schreuders, who lives in Amsterdam, started his first magazine,
De Wolkenkrabber (The Skyscraper), in 1971. This necessitated his becoming
a graphic designer, which has been his profession ever since. Other magazines
followed:* De Poezenkrant *and* Furore. *He is the art director for the weekly* VPRO Gids
*magazine and the music label Basta, and has written books about graphic design,
paperback covers, and the Beatles.*

Did you start your career as a graphic designer?
Yes, you could say that, although those design activities
began as so many things I undertook as a hobby, which
then became a passion and/or a profession. I started
doing magazines (*De Wolkenkrabber, De Poezenkrant,
Furore*) as a student, not as a way to make money. Then
clients started to come to me and everything seemed to
evolve from there, almost by itself. By age 25, I was a full-
time freelance designer, and this profession has supported
my family and myself ever since.

**You've produced books, magazines, and music.
What do you think ties all these activities together?**
My interest in popular culture, in its broadest sense,
because it ties the people of the world together. So what
better subject is there for books, magazines, and music?

**The music you've helped produce and package
for the band called the Beau Hunks comes from
years of incredible research. Clearly, it is an act
of passion. But do you also build profit into this
equation? Do you produce these products to make
money?**
With the Beau Hunks projects, I actually made a little
money by listing myself as coarranger of the songs I
reconstructed, so every year some royalties come in.
The Beau Hunks are a business partnership consisting
of Frank van Balen (financial advice), Gert-Jan Blom
(orchestra leader), and myself (research and design). As

The Beau Hunks, we license our recordings to record or
film companies. And as a designer of the CD packages,
I charged my regular fee. All of this doesn't amount to
much, but the main reward is hearing that wonderful
music and sharing it with the world.

**Given your distinctive practice, which is not
devoted to serving clients but rather yourself,
I would call you an entrepreneur. Would you
agree?**
Well, I don't quite agree with the first part of your
statement, since most of my time is devoted to serving
clients. I am art director of *VPRO Gids* magazine two
days a week and do freelance design jobs two days
a week. The projects I undertake as "entrepreneur"
are squeezed in between those jobs. I wish I could do
more books, documentary films, or magazine projects,
but time just doesn't allow it. The latest issue of *De
Poezenkrant* (#52), for instance, took me twenty two
months to put together.

**If we can agree that you do entrepreneurial
activities, how much of this is dependent on your
skill and craft as a designer?**
I think I use my design skills to tie the various elements
in a project together. This happens after a long period
of studying the raw materials, spending a lot of time
with it, and trying to really understand it until I have
a feeling for the subject, and then the design sort of

These CD covers showcasing the tunes of Leroy Shield performed by The Beau Hunks have been an ongoing exploration into movie music. Design: Schreuders.

takes care of itself. The design skill is there all along, but it comes in last in the production flow.

You've published your own magazine, _FURORE_, for many years. Do you work this on a business model, or is it an intuitive urge?
It comes out of an authentic, intuitive urge, definitely. _Furore_ started because of an intense desire to write and design a magazine. Ideally, it would have to be the best in the world. In 1974, I had been working as an assistant layout/paste-up man for an underground magazine (_Aloha_) for two years. I also enjoyed writing articles. When _Aloha_ stopped publishing, I got together with a group of like-minded individuals, and we started _Furore_ magazine. Unfortunately, none of us had any business sense whatsoever. As a result, the halls, attic, and bike shed of my home are full of boxes of unsold back issues of _Furore_. But I'm not complaining. Whenever an issue appears, at least 1,000 copies are sold, sometimes more. This is usually enough to cover expenses.

Knowing your penchant for uncovering and documenting the rare, and obscure, and thereby making them popular, is there an area of popular culture that you are anxious to enter that you have not already?
This is very hard to say, because new subjects have a habit of sneaking up on you when you're not paying attention. And some subjects have a habit of returning to me time and again with long intervals in between. For instance, I first wrote about paperback cover art in 1981, returned to it in 1991, made a documentary about cover artist James Avati in 2000, and wrote a book about him in 2005. Although I really try to say everything I want to in a publication, there's always more that needs to be said as the years go by. The same happened with the Leroy Shield music project. I thought that was finished by 1993, but we were still at it in 2007.

That's the price of obsession.
In 1982, I decided to do a book about early Beatles photographs. I estimated this would take me about two years of research and another year to write. But I am still researching it in 2007 and I fear I may never actually write it. Along the way, however, I did amass a wealth of knowledge, which I have been able to share with other (more productive) authors. I also cowrote a book on Beatles locations (with Mark Lewisohn and Adam Smith), which was published in 1994 and quickly sold out. This summer, we will be working on the revised and expanded edition. Projects like this never stop, it seems.

Cover for the quirky _De Poezenkrant_ Issue # 52, featuring Felix-Katten, a feline star. Design: Schreuders.

{ CARLOS SEGURA

T26, DIGITAL TYPE FOUNDRY

Carlos Segura is the founder of T26 Digital Type Foundry. He is a designer and art director who has created many fonts and has started over five companies including an independent record label, Thickface. Segura Inc. is now two ventures, one that deals with print-related projects and Segura Interactive, which focuses on new media.

How and why did you start T26?

It all started in 1991 with the font Neo, that I designed for a project in Chicago. We received so many calls inquiring if it was for sale that I started thinking of what to do with it. But it was three years later when we actually started the foundry. We were very conscientious of starting something truly different, of wanting to offer new ways of thinking in the font industry beyond aesthetics. Keep in mind that this was before the Internet. If you were a designer in those days and you needed to do research on experimental typography, or style comparisons, or even availability, it was quite a chore. We wanted to create a resource for those who were seeking forward-thinking font designs and a venue for type designers who wanted to offer new creations. We were the first to promote our fonts with motion graphics in the form of QuickTime movies, like music videos. In terms of printed promotions, we made a conscious effort to create our "font kits" as limited edition "gift packages" instead of making them feel like a marketing tool. In each font kit we included our posters, postcards, books, catalogs, napkins, buttons, and so on all produced in varied techniques like silkscreen, offset, letterpress, linoleum cuts, original art, and so on. Each kit had a 3,000-unit run and once it was gone, we would start over from scratch.

With all the fonts available free on the Web, how does T26 justify its existence to its customers?

We first need to differentiate the font foundries from the free-font sites, and this distinction lies primarily in the quality of the product and the accountability of the source. The free fonts you'll find on the Web are usually of poor design, both aesthetically and technically. Beyond the visual aspects, there's a lot that goes into the development and construction of a digital font that a free site can't offer. If they did provide the necessary attention to their work, they wouldn't be giving it away.

Are most of your faces licensed, or do you create the majority yourself?

It's a little of both.

In the grunge age of the 1990s, many of your T26 faces took on that quality. Now they run a sophisticated gamut from functional to decorative. How do you determine what your products will be?

There is an incredible amount of compromises that come into play, from style, design, family size, and price to technical perfection, compatibility, formats, character set, languages, and personal taste. Stylistically speaking, it's hard to predict. We still see great success with a variety of our oldest fonts. Predicting a new development or even a

T26 Digital Type Foundry is a pioneer in contemporary type and typography. In this poster they show off their eclectic wares. Design: Segura Inc.

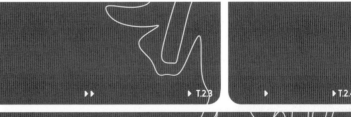

One of T26's font kits made to give the aura of a limited edition gift package. Each includes posters, postcards, books, buttons, and all manner of ephemera. Design: T26.

T.2.3

T.2.4

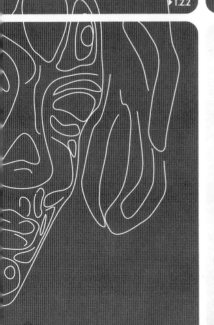

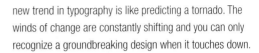

new trend in typography is like predicting a tornado. The winds of change are constantly shifting and you can only recognize a groundbreaking design when it touches down.

What are your biggest sellers? And who is your audience?
There are quite a few that are constantly performing well, but as a general rule, we find script and san serif fonts to dominate sales.

How much of your time is devoted to T26?
A lot, but we also have dedicated staff just for that venture.

Do you consider yourself an entrepreneur in the sense that you have vision and are taking risk?
Most certainly! If it weren't for the Segura design firm and our personal commitment to the brand and our field, T26 would not have made it alone.

Promotional poster for a futuristic font called Spaceships by TNOP for T26.

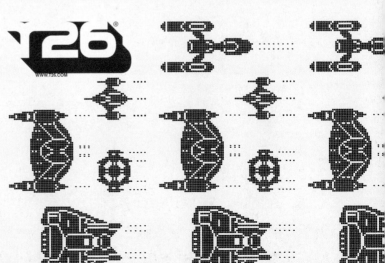

{ MIKE MILLS
THE HUMANS PROJECT

Mike Mills is a filmmaker, graphic designer, and artist. As a filmmaker, he has completed music videos, commercials, short films, documentaries, and the feature film Thumbsucker in 2005. Mills cofounded The Directors Bureau in 1996, a multidisciplinary production company. His design work includes campaigns for clients such as Levis, Gap, Volkswagen, and Nike.

You are, well, a polymath—a graphic, textile, product designer, filmmaker, and writer. Why so many endeavors?

Raised in the 1970s, I was inundated by a mixed-media world. Characters and themes were spread across many different forms: A TV show had a toy connected to the show, and the graphics on the toy box and the feeling of the theme music for that show were all connected. I was interested in that whole world, more than one aspect of it. I think more and more people will have careers like mine in the future. My biggest influences when I was in college were Charles and Ray Eames, Herbert Bayer, the conceptual artist Hans Haacke, and artists like Fischli and Weiss. All these people do all sorts of things and have a built-in critique of the false professional categories between artist, designer, filmmaker, architect, painter, sculptor, and photographer. I don't think I am doing all sorts of different things; I think I'm doing the same project in different ways. Also, the categories you listed are different than I would use to describe myself. I'm a graphic designer and a filmmaker. If I did some textiles, that's just part of being a designer. If I write, that's just part of being a filmmaker.

Years ago, you wrote about the Bauhaus and Herbert Bayer. Are you kind of living out the Bauhaus ideals of the Total Work of Art in the present tense?

Yes, also the ideals of the Werner Werkstatt, the Arts and Crafts, and the Constructivists. They all believed that our domestic world could be a place of high thought and heightened experience, a revolutionary place. Also, all those projects sought to get past the rarified, segregated position or traditional gallery- and museum-based art. In this way, I think of the Bauhaus and Fluxus and even the Situationist together. In different ways, they were trying to get out of the controlled theater of the art world and away from the "aura" of art. They hoped to be more powerful and more subversive by being part of mainstream, even consumer society. Most those projects have a leftist/ Marxist ideological basis to them, which I admire, but my interests are more personal. I'm concerned with how the large societal forces are at play in our internal, subjective, and emotional lives. My posters, and scarves, and ribbons are speaking to that internal place, where our history, myths, power struggles, and psychological struggles take place.

What exactly is Humans? And what is your goal in developing this line?

The Humans project imbeds highly personal themes into mass-produced items such as posters, scarves, ribbons, fabric patterns, T-shirts, and bags. Humans operates in between the art world and popular culture, in between graphic design and an art practice. I wanted to make things that had the possibility of interaction, the fabrics and ribbons, things that were cheap and part of everyday life, and things that were expendable.

Why do you call it Humans?

At one point, I wanted to call it "Thumbsucker Humans" because, basically, that's what the film is about. And basically, that's what all my work is about: dealing with the frailties of being human, trying to be more human (vulnerable, alive, relaxed) by making things, and trying to reach and communicate with other humans through what I make.

Did you have to create a unique business plan to handle Humans?

I was lucky to have a very nice team of Japanese people believe in my work, and I wanted to make something special. You will not find a culture more sympathetic to design or more sensitive viewers. I think Japanese culture has long fostered appreciation, reading, connoisseurship, and buying things as a form of self-authorship. We have no stellar business plan besides making it as cheap as possible and stay small. We are not very professional in terms of marketing, sales, and strategy, which gives me great hope.

What products are unique to Humans that would not be in your repertoire otherwise?

Almost all my graphic work is now just for Humans. I try to put all my graphic eggs in that basket for now, attempting to create as large and as deep a body of work as I can. So often, being a designer, you go from here to there, this theme to that one, this issue to that, this client to that. Humans is the opposite of that.

The patterns you create are so bright and sunny. What influences the Humans line?

Actually, many of the themes behind the work are actually fairly dark. Humans 02 was created just after my father died and is all about that experience. I've always been interested in contradictory exteriors and interiors, in the connection between happy and sad. Sometimes my work is apparently sunny while I am critiquing that imagery, and sometimes my work is sunny because I'm desperately trying to be positive about life, but it's rarely just sunny.

Fashions from the Humans project, which conflates highly personal themes into mass-produced items. Clothes designed by Susan Ciancialo, "Queen of Hearts" collection, using Humans fabrics designed by Mike Mills; photos by Maggie Manzer.

One of many pattern designs, titled
Plate Crack created by Mills.

Another pattern design, titled *Marks Paper Ribbons* designed by Mills.

{ JULIAN MONTAGUE

THE STRAY SHOPPING CART PROJECT

Julian Montague is a Buffalo, New York–based artist and graphic designer. His work includes several visually dissimilar projects that use drawing, photography, and graphic design to explore the ways in which scientific classification constructs meaning and imposes order through language. His book, The Stray Shopping Carts of Eastern North America: A Guide to Field Identification, *published by Abrams in 2006, is the marriage of conceptual art and informational design. Montague is also represented by Black & White Gallery in New York City.*

How did the shopping cart book project start? What was your motivation?

The idea for the project came about several years ago. I was driving through an intersection near where I live in Buffalo and I noticed that there were shopping carts on people's lawns, at bus stops turned up side down, and so forth. I thought that there might be something interesting to be done on the subject. However, I knew that if I simply took photographs of stray shopping carts, the images would only read as a sort of sad urban commentary that would not be much different than your average college kid's social documentary photo project. I decided to try to figure out what happened to stray shopping carts by observing them in the way a naturalist might observe the behavior of a wild animal. This approach led to a rudimentary system of classification that named and defined the different states in which a stray shopping cart might be found. The project first appeared as a two-page spread in a Buffalo zine called *Basta!*

As I worked on the project and learned more about the movements of stray shopping carts, my taxonomy became more refined and carefully thought out. It quickly became clear that what was interesting about the project was the way that I could sensitize my viewers to the presence of stray carts. People would often tell me that after seeing my work they started seeing shopping carts everywhere. By using such a thoroughly detailed vocabulary to describe a mundane phenomenon, I was

able—to a small degree—to make viewers see, in the peripheries of the urban landscape, what had previously been invisible. The project for me became less about shopping carts and more about the way in which scientific

Obsession underscores this highly personal project titled Stray Shopping Carts by Julian Montague.

classification constructs meaning and imposes order through language. I never pose carts or set up situations.

You published your book through Abrams. Why didn't you do it yourself?
I did not have the means on my own to produce and distribute the book in the way that I would have wanted. But more importantly, Abrams allowed me to design the book myself, so I did not feel that I had to compromise my vision. The single change I had to make was that I originally wanted to use a dark brown on the cover and the marketing department told me that brown on a book cover violated a tried and true rule of publishing.

Is there a problem in thinking of an audience for art? Isn't that the opposite of what art is about?
I do not think that there is a problem in thinking about an audience for art. Perhaps, for some artists, art is about uncompromisingly depicting their inner life without caring whether or not anybody else can understand it. But I think

the majority of artists are trying to communicate in some meaningful way with their viewers, whether emotionally, politically, aesthetically, or whatever.

The art world today, from museum to individuals, is thinking more about selling products (or artifacts). Where is the line between this and the mainstream?
I think that there is a line. On one side of the line you have a necktie depicting Van Gogh's *Starry Night* and on the other side you have the artist Marcel Dzama's action figures. The Van Gogh tie adds nothing to one's appreciation of *Starry Night,* and it does not work particularly well as an ironic comment or as a conceptual joke. The tie exists only to be given as a gift and to serve as proof that the giver has visited a museum. Marcel Dzama's action figures (and other artist-designed toys), on the other hand, are a legitimate extension of an artist's sensibilities into mass-produced objects. The toys exist as art objects in their own right and have the added benefit of being affordable in a way that paintings are not.

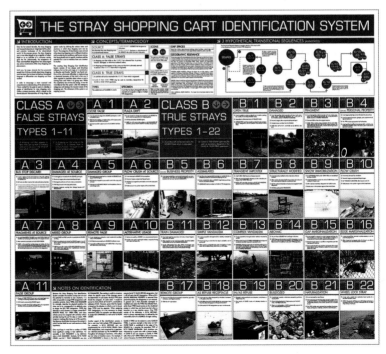

Detail and spread from the book *Stray Shopping Carts*, which denotes a system of classification that names and defines the different states in which a stray shopping cart might be found. Design: Montague.

THE REAL EMPIRES OF EVIL

BURGER KINGDOM

DEBTMARK

IRONY COAST

CAN-ADA

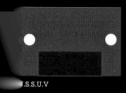

U.S.S.U.V

NOSMOKIA

SPILLED MARTINIQUE

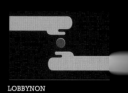

LOBBYNON

EXECUTIVE SALARIA

ECONOMIA

SCAN-DINAVIA

N.R.ASIA

UNITED STATES OF FLORIDA

DENTALIBAN

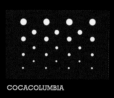

COCACOLUMBIA

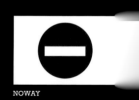

NOWAY

FINLAND

UNITED STATES OF AMNESIA

WORKING OVERTIMOR

"KUWAITER!"

HUNGERY

LA-LA-LAND

SUDANDRUFF

CONFED. OF RUSSIAN NOVELS

When illustrator Christoph Neimann puts his mind to satire he is unstoppable. His "The Real Empires of Evil" flags were produced on his own for the publication *NoZone:Empire*, edited by Nicolas Blechman.

{ CHRISTOPH NIEMANN

100% EVIL

C hristoph Niemann is an illustrator, animator, and graphic designer who lives and works in both New York City and Berlin. His work appears regularly on the covers of the New York Times Magazine, The New Yorker, Atlantic Monthly, *and* Newsweek. *In addition to his* 100% *series, he also authors and illustrates books for children; his first was* The Police Cloud.

Do you consider yourself an illustrator, designer, or man-about-town?
By education and approach, I belong firmly in the design camp, but since 90 percent of what I do qualifies as illustration, I guess illustrator is more appropriate.

How much of your illustration work is self-generated? In other words, how much do you just sit around and draw with the goal of putting something together that is totally your own?
Of the work that ends up as dollars in my account, probably 95 percent is assignments. Working on children's books is the only real entrepreneurial work I do that has the potential to generate money. But even though projects like the *100%* book series are money pits, they are inseparable from my overall business strategy, as far as generating new directions and styles and, of course, attracting more people to what we do.

The *100%* book series is a collaboration with my dear friend Nicholas Blechman.

So, how did *100% Evil* evolve?
I had always done little concept books, very small editions just for myself or to give out to a couple of friends and colleagues. Nicholas had a lot more publication experience, having edited a good numbers of issues of *NoZone* (his political illustration/comic fanzine), but has also been a long-time fan of small-edition drawing books. So we decided to start a monothematic artist book series,

just 100 copies in various sizes and techniques. The idea was to sell each book for one percent of the production price, so it was designed to be absolutely nonprofit. After three issues, we were tired of putting so much work into the book and then only having so few copies to give out that we decided to work with a real publisher, Princeton Architectural Press. This, of course, killed our original concept, but we still don't make any money on it (our book release party cost at least twice the amount of our advance), so we certainly stayed true to the nonprofit idea.

Do you think of an audience when you produce your entrepreneurial work?
I have to admit I always think of my audience when I work, which may be my biggest strength and my biggest weakness. When it comes to the *100%* books though, we don't drive ourselves crazy over the thought of a reader not getting every single joke right away.

You've recently stepped over to the dark side of children's books. Do you see this as a new entrepreneurial outlet?
Quite frankly, I think this is much more of an entre-preneurial outlet than the *100%* books. I can't claim that I have any thorough knowledge about the publishing world and despite some fairly warm reviews, I doubt that *The Police Cloud* will put any of my kids through college—not even a very small college. Nonetheless, there is at least the theoretical possibility to turn a children's book into

I have to admit I always think of my audience when I work, which may be my biggest strength and my biggest weakness.

something larger, more complex, like plastic toys, a TV series, movie rights, Tom Hanks asking me to play the lead, Niemann Theme Park and Resort...the usual.

But seriously, even though right now I have a solid amount of work from editorial clients, I know that there is no federal law that guarantees me a perpetual stream of assignments from magazines. So I think it would be professional suicide not to try out new things. I am convinced that you have to constantly look for new outlets and entrepreneurial directions. Once your bread-and-butter clients turn away from you, it is too late—you have to start looking for new possibilities when you can, not when you have to.

100% Love. **Do you have a goal in mind with this?**
Creative bliss. I have no problems with the restrictions that I have to deal with when working on assigned projects, but as you become a bit smarter about what works and what doesn't, you inevitably start to subconsciously self-censor. Working on self-generated projects like the *100%* series takes away all the excuses and forces you to think very hard about what it is that you really want. I think this is

extremely important if you want to be in this profession for the long haul.

I know this is a terrible question, but how do you get your ideas?
Very simple: getting up (relatively) early, sitting at a desk with plenty of white paper and pencils, no music, and then thinking until my head hurts. Every once in a while a nice idea just flies at me in the subway or while reading the paper, but unfortunately that happens very rarely. My rule is, "no pain, no gain."

Do you plan on developing more content, or are you content responding to manuscripts?
I illustrated another children's book that was written by Stephen J. Dubner. I really like the story, and Stephen is terrific to work with, so the whole experience couldn't have been better. That said, I am not very keen on illustrating other people's stories. I see my strengths in working on both the conceptual part and the execution, and I'm not real interested in visually acting out somebody else's jokes.

(Left) Illustrations from
100% Evil and (right)
100% Love by Niemann
and Nicholas Blechman,
edition 1 of 100
silkscreened books.

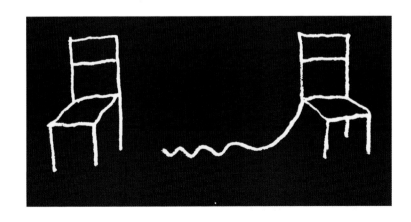

{ JOHN BIGELOW TAYLOR & DIANNE DUBLER

KUBABA BOOKS

John Bigelow Taylor and Dianne Dubler have traveled around the world to photograph art objects, paintings, jewelry, sculpture, architecture, and architectural interiors. They have also curated exhibitions and produced films. In 1991, they founded Kubaba, a publishing company to design and author limited-edition photography books.

Both of you pursued your photographic careers while living in Afghanistan, India, and Nepal in the 1970s. Your focus was on these exotic realms, documenting culture, antiquity, and so on. Why did this become your focal point?

DD: Travel and a curiosity about other cultures were the initial incentives to hit the road. The first Asian journey was inspired, in particular, by seeing an image of the Buddhas of Bamiyan (now destroyed by the Taliban) in Afghanistan. This was the early 1970s, and there was a movement of many young Western people from North America and Europe to Asia—drawn by stories from those recently returned as well as by counter-culture literature. Once there, we encountered and became deeply involved with Tibetan refugees, monks, Lamas, Indian Yogis, Sufi sheiks, and a large family of Western travelers who continually expanded our consciousness and experience. Our lives would be forever spiritually transformed. It is also interesting to note that this "family," while dispersed worldwide, is in constant communication.

You've both created images for almost a hundred books and many through a relationship with the publishing house of Harry N. Abrams. At what point did this evolve from more than an "assignment" into creating content for your own books?

JBT: It grew out of our relationships with clients, who in several cases wanted to self-publish books on their art-related material. We felt we had gained a certain amount of experience through working on a number of books by

that point and were excited about putting our own creative ideas into practice. We had worked on a small book on the Japanese collection at the Newark Museum with Kuan Chang (now an accomplished artist) who became an early collaborator in our publishing endeavors.

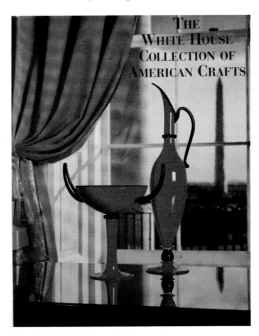

(Left) The Dalai Lama in meditation in Central Park, 1991. Photograph: Taylor and Dubler.

(Above) Cover of *The White House Collection of American Craft.* Photographed and styled by Taylor and Dubler in 1995.

(Left) Front cover of *Maraini: Acts of Photography, Acts of Love*, conceived, designed and produced by Kubaba Books in 2000.

(Below left) Cover of *The Splendor of Ethnic Jewelry*, project originated and photographed by Taylor and Dubler in 1994.

(Below right) Cover of *Transformations*, conceived, photographed, designed and produced as the first Kubaba Books project in 1989.

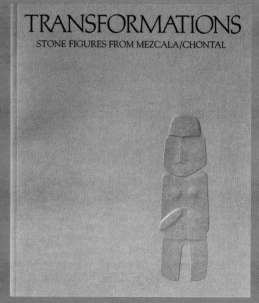

Your own book packaging company is called Kubaba Books, which you founded in 1991. First, what does Kubaba mean?

DD: Kubaba was the earliest Indo-European name for the great mother-goddess of Anatolia. The name is formed from the Indian goddess named "Kunti" and the male honorific "baba," as Kubaba was a self-generating deity. She goes on to Greece as Cybele and to Rome as Diana.

How much of your energies are devoted to this entrepreneurial venture?

DD + JBT: We are usually involved in one Kubaba project at a time, which can last from a couple of months to a couple of years or more. The projects are becoming more and more of our own development rather than publishing the work of others.

Did you have a business model when you began, or did it emerge as a kind of impromptu, if not logical, result of your photographic business?

DD: No business model at all. For our first project, we had a client who had assembled a collection of pre-Columbian art they wanted to sell. We proposed to them to create a book as an elegant sales tool. We photographed their collection, designed the book, and oversaw the entire printing and production.

How deeply does Kubaba Books get involved with all aspects of the book business, from conception to production to distribution?

JBT: To date, we have avoided distribution completely. Other than that, we are totally involved in every other aspect. And we've done not only books; we have curated photographic exhibitions and produced and directed a film as well.

What have been your most successful titles?

JBT: Probably *Fosco Maraini: Acts of Photography, Acts of Love*. Maraini was an Italian photographer, mountaineer,

Japan scholar, anthropologist, writer, filmmaker, and professor. He became the subject of a book and film, all designed, produced, and directed by Kubaba, and a photographic exhibition, cocurated with Mikio Shinagawa and shown in his gallery in New York. Another major project developed entirely by us—though not published by Kubaba—was a book on tribal jewelry called, The *Splendor of Ethnic Jewelry*. This was based on an important collection in Belgium, which, working with the owners, we shaped into an encyclopedic volume, initially published in the United States by Abrams and later in German and French editions with other publishers.

Since success is often a relative term, what is your most satisfying title?

DD + JBT: Certainly the Maraini book. He was a larger-than-life figure, but modest and rather quiet. In fact, the title of our film is, *Silently Drawn*. He came from the old world of true erudition and massive accomplishments, so he had no need to hype himself. He was the photographer on the Italian expeditions to Tibet in 1937 and 1948, led Italian mountaineering expeditions in the Karakorum and Hindu Kush, and became a leading anthropologist of the Ainu, the indigenous culture of northern Japan. *Secret Tibet* and *Meeting with Japan* remain two of the most important books on these subjects. We created this project because, other than to a select few groups of Tibet and Japan scholars and international mountaineers, he was unknown in America. He was a "teacher" in the Eastern sense, by the example of the life he led.

What does Kubaba allow you to do that simply working as assignment photographers does not?

JBT: It gives us absolute freedom to exercise our vision in whatever project we are involved.

{ TJEERD VEENHOVEN

PADDED WALL TILES

T*jeerd Veenhoven studied at Arnhem school (The Kogeschool voor de Kunsten HKU) in The Netherlands. Upon graduation in 2000, he founded his design studio in Groningen, Holland, where he designs products, exhibitions, furniture, and large tents for festivals and exhibitions.*

When did you become a design entrepreneur? And what was your first project that did not stem from a client?

I have been designing my own collection from the start. I was lucky enough to have clients who just wanted something that I designed. I didn't really design according to specifications; it always turned into something my clients never expected. But there is always some sort of influence by clients, therefore I almost never exhibit these projects, not even on my website. I only publish the projects that originate from me and only me.

Was it a leap to go from client-driven work to your own?

Of course, the most difficult thing is the money. If you want to do special projects and you are always trying to innovate, then you have to accept that you spend way too much time and money on research and development, something you can not have your private clients pay for. For me, it is far more important to implement my own ideas in these projects. Everything you design should have something to do with your own work, even if it is just a little. I often experiment on the projects I do for clients in order to be able to further develop a design after finishing the project.

The Padded Wall Tile designed for a client who commissioned a large upholstered storage cupboard in his bedroom, which became an entrepreneurial product.

One of your projects is the Padded Wall. What made you conceive this as an entrepreneurial project?

The Padded Wall Tile is a perfect example of this. A private client wanted his large storage cupboard in his bedroom upholstered (over 90 meters). They saw the foam wall-tiles I engineered and designed for a restaurant in Groningen and wanted the same thing, but I wasn't really interested in doing that again, so I came up with the Padded Wall Tile. Even though their budget didn't cover the research and development, I took the challenge anyway. The project took me four months to complete instead of the two months planned. The costs tripled and I eventually only got paid for the materials and my employees. But with all this knowledge, I was convinced that it could be a product with a promising future, so I went and looked for a design label that was interested. Zuiver (www.zuiver.eu) took on the challenge to make this product commercial and it's now a big hit. This was possible because I had done so much research, so it was relatively easy for them to find a producer. Now the product is distributed worldwide; it was well worth the effort and the costs.

What did you have to learn?

I have learned a lot about materials, adhesives, and things you generally need to know about producing something. This is one of my better qualities. But I like to see it more in the philosophical way: I had to learn everything; I didn't know squat. The only thing I had was my design philosophy, rooted in being playful. I believe I should not become too self-aware because naiveté allows me to be original.

How much did you invest in this and what has been the return?

It was a very costly project—it took so much time and energy. The greatest thing is that my client was so impressed by the way I kept going and not giving up. It made him aware that he owned something very special. And even though the same tile is being mass-produced, he knows he has the first, the genesis project. And I think that is one of the greater rewards—a very intense relationship with your clients. Their appreciation is the most important thing to me.

You've been working on Hard Coated Foam for seven years. What is this project all about?

The Hard Coated Foam is an ongoing development of a new material. A long time ago, I would spend my Sundays melting EPS foam in my frying pan—don't ask me why, I can't remember. The result was interesting enough to further develop the results. Melting and compressing foam on a custom-designed and built oven forms a hard top layer on the foam, in which optional reinforcements can be melted. This all resulted in a strong sandwich panel, which can be customized to specifications (for instance, on one side, a Kevlar fiber is melted and imbedded while the other side is reinforced with a decorative material).

The great thing is that the sandwich panel, apart from the reinforcements, is made from one single material type (EPS-foam), which makes it much easier to recycle. Also, there is no need for unfriendly adhesives to bind the layers as in conventional sandwich panels and no need for a topcoat or any other finish. It is patented and picked up by several companies for further development. This takes forever, and it will take another five years before it will be applied to products.

The Padded Wall took on a life of it's own and was costly too. These are details showing the wall's various interior applications. Design: Tjeerd Veenhoven.

{ JAMES VICTORE

VICTORE PLATES

James Victore is a designer who claims his studio is hell-bent on world domination. Clients include Amnesty International, the New York Times, MTV, Target, Moet & Chandon, and the Shakespeare Project. He is an Emmy-award winner for television animation, a Gold Medalist from the Broadcast Designers Association, and the recipient of a Grand Prix from the Brno Biennale (Czech Republic).

What influenced you to start doing illustrated plates?

I have been drawing on plates since I was 22 and spending time in bars and restaurants. I always carry markers and paint pens with me. I don't know what possessed me to pick up a plate and draw on it. Maybe it was the wine. I was in a restaurant in Barcelona recently with Laura and friends, and I happened to have a paint marker with me. I made two plates, three bottles, and painted Hillman Curtis' cell phone. This is my preferred way to work.

Did you envision this as an entrepreneurial venture or just another way of making design/art?

The first plates were just made to give away. I'd give them to friends, waiters, and cute girls. There was no other concern, certainly not about getting paid for them. I have none of them; I gave them all away. But I saw one recently in a friend's house and was really attracted to it until I recognized it as mine.

How did you get them into Design Within Reach (DWR)? And how have they succeeded?

The DWR connection came from my first small show at Paul Weston's gallery in Brooklyn. I sent invitations to all my friends, one of who happened to be Ray Brunner, vice president of DWR, who immediately called and said, "This looks like fun. Can you do it for us?" The show went well, was extended from one month to three. Out of one hundred plates, we sold almost half.

Picasso was a big plate maker. What were some of your influences?

I first visited the Picasso museum in Paris when I was twenty-eight. I had no idea before then that he made plates. I was completely moved by his pottery. They are still some of my favorite Picasso works—they have an immediacy and feel, and look like the act of creation. I also love Fornasetti. I've known of his work since I was a kid, although it's much more stagnant than Picasso's work.

Let's talk nitty-gritty. How do you go about deciding on designs and then bringing them to fruition?

This is the crux of my problem. I am not really interested in making a rubber stamp of two bunnies having sex and then having it printed on 1,000 plates, although the money might be good. I want to make 100 different plates and have them all be unique and usable. But I am not a potter. I'm a designer. I work like a designer. We are working on a limited edition for DWR right now.

Limited-edition Victore plates designed as gifts for "friends, waiters, and cute girls."
Design: James Victore

More plates in Victore's series illustrating his obsessive passion for carnal love and politics.

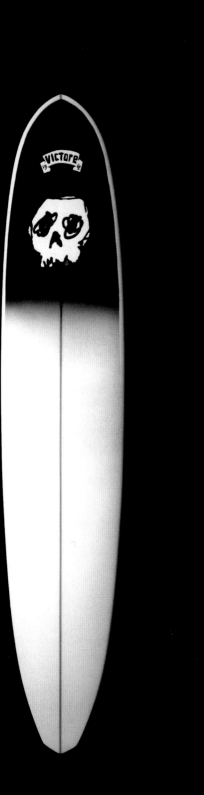

How many do you make at a time? And are all these limited edition?
I make them when I think of them, one at a time. Yes, they are all limited to one or two editions. The plate that reads, "I love NY more than Milton Glaser," is very popular among designers. I have made three or maybe four.

What has been the biggest plate challenge, artistically and technically, for you?
I am trying to figure out the multiples thing. I like the idea of more people having my work, but I still want it to be fresh and exciting. And moving from "art piece" to usable dinner plates is the goal.

Do you foresee this as being a small part of a larger entrepreneurial business?
I don't concern myself with the business end. I probably should, but I let the universe take care of that for me. It thrills me to know that folks are interested in the things I make.

Are you going to break the plate mold? What's next?
I am creating a limited edition of surfboards. I have five that I am painting and will post for sale or try to find a little show for them. Right now these are my pet project. They are very sexy; I may just use them all myself.

Limited-edition
surfboard, one in a
series of five of Victore's
current "pet projects"
soon to be in production.
Design: Victore

Follow your bliss.

{ LAURA VICTORE

FORTUNE COOKIE PURSE AND BOO RALEY LADY BUDS

*L*aura Victore, a freelance designer and illustrator in New York, was a design student at the School of Visual Arts when she conceived and produced a unique line of gift items. Working out of her studio in Brooklyn, she's developed change purses and earrings that are currently sold at museum stores.

What made you conceive of a fortune cookie purse?

I was in my senior year at SVA studying under Paul Sahre and my thesis project for the year was "Gift." A gift is something that makes you feel good and makes you want to share that feeling with others. A fortune cookie is a perfect example. Besides the ingenious simplicity of its design (a folded circle), there is a wonderful sense of surprise that comes with the ritual opening of them after a nice meal. The cookie is a gift. You don't pay for it. And then, once you open the tiny edible package, you receive a forecast or positive message, and you instantly want to share your fortune with everyone around you.

Was materiality an important concern for you?

I've always been drawn to 3-D. It's more fun to get my hands dirty and create an actual object that someone can hold or interact with. I was doing a lot of experimenting with materials and packaging. Playing in the studio with some scrap leather, I sewed together a rough prototype for a small purse in the shape of a fortune cookie. Once I realized the pattern was a circle, I immediately thought, "Hey! I could put a zipper along the edge and make a cute little bag!"

Once you made prototypes, what did you know or have to learn to bring the product to market?

I don't have any kind of business background (and they don't teach you these things in art school, which I think is a great misfortune and missed opportunity), so I just jumped into it and made all sorts of mistakes. But the other side of that naiveté is that sometimes you take bigger risks because you don't know any other way and then you reap higher rewards.

But the biggest trepidation is…?

Fighting off the fear that I have absolutely no idea what I'm doing. Looking back on the cookie coin purse, I'm amazed that I got it into big stores like Takashimaya and MoMA Design Store. I just called them up and asked if I could have the buyer's address so I could send them a sample. It's wild. Now I'm reading all sorts of books about setting up your business correctly, budgeting, marketing, sourcing, production, distribution, QuickBooks, patent law, and e-commerce.

Tell me about the Boo Raley Lady Buds?

They are earplug earrings, a fashionable accessory that also provides convenient and high-quality ear protection. They've got beauty and brains, which is a pretty sexy combination. They were made for women who go to NASCAR races.

Is this just an intuitive project, or did you do some research to see whether the world wanted it?

I did a little research and found that the noise levels of races like NASCAR and Formula One, not to mention rock concerts and nightclubbing, are way above the level our ears should be exposed to. And here's the clincher: Noise-induced hearing loss is permanent. That's just scary and no fun at all! I thought it was crazy that the majority of people there didn't have any ear protection. I realized that conventional earplugs have this stigma of being dorky looking and hard to keep track of. So we combined a chic looking earring with a high-quality, reusable earplug *et voilá!* Now women everywhere can be fashionable and protect their ears all in one powerful swoop.

(Left) The fortune cookie purse was conceived when Laura Victore was a senior at the School of Visual Arts; (right) The Boo Raley Buds are a fashion accessory for women who attend frequent NASCAR races. Design: Laura Victore.

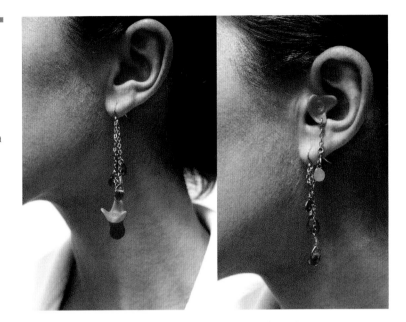

(Above) An alternate style of the fortune cookie purse and the small fortune coin purse fashioned after a take-out food container. Design: Victore. Cookie coin purse photos: Davies & Starr.

UNDER CONSIDERATION
EST. 2001

A growing network and enterprise dedicated to the progress of the graphic design profession and its practitioners, students and enthusiasts. At times intangible, its purpose is to question, push, analyze and agitate graphic design and those involved in the profession. *More about UnderConsideration...*

THINGS TO DO AROUND HERE

1 / You could learn about the hard-working founders
2 / Peruse a list of current contributors
3 / Get an idea of what our 3 x 3 advertising is all about
4 / Or just enjoy the lively sites that make up this corner of the internet by scrolling down, reading and clicking where necessary

THE UNDERCONSIDERATION ONLINE NETWORK / INFO + RECENT ACTIVITY

Speak Up
Q UIPSOLOGIES

undercorsideration.com/speakup
Discussing, and looking for, what is relevant in, and the relevance of, graphic design.
More about Speak Up...

undercorsideration.com/quipsologies
Corralling the most relevant and creative on- and off-line bits that pertain to the design community.
More about Quipsologies...

RECENT ACTIVITY | RSS

A Texas Dramedy
Posted on Jul.25.2007 by Armin

Qs / Vol. 7 / July.16 - July.22
Posted on Jul.23.2007 by Speak Up

Dark and Fleshy: The Color of Top Grossing Movies
Posted on Jul.17.2007 by Armin

Qs / Vol. 7 / July.9 - July.15
Posted on Jul.16.2007 by Speak Up

Madvertising
Posted on Jul.12.2007 by Jason A. Tselentis

RECENT ACTIVITY / RSS AUTHORS, COMMUNITY

Quipsologies | From the Authors

Vol. 7 | No. 67
"Admitting that I find process slides a chore is one [...]

Vol. 7 | No. 66
Wes Anderson you silly boy, credits go at the bottom [...]

Vol. 7 | No. 65
Freelancers Union has gone national and they're sponsoring a Meet [...]

Vol. 7 | No. 64
The most expensive behind the scenes ever: Damien Hirst's $90,000,000+ [...]

Vol. 7 | No. 63
To second Motiongrapher's thoughts: "Dope type animation".

Quipsologies | From the Community

Vol. 7 | No. 90
Related to Armin's Quip. No. 66â€¦ Trailer for Wes [...]

Vol. 7 | No. 89
Video-game designer and filmmaker Theresa Duncan has committed suicide. Her [...]

Vol. 7 | No. 88
'Old media' content remains king. Ha! VR/ Quipped [...]

Vol. 7 | No. 87
Classic movie robots. VR/ Quipped by Joe Moran [...]

Vol. 7 | No. 86
Helvetica 50th anniversary cake. Ala Steve Zissou! Non? [...]

BRAND NEW

undercorsideration.com/brandnew
Displaying opinions, and focusing solely on corporate and brand identity work.
More about Brand New...

RECENT ACTIVITY / RSS

The Kangaroo With More Power
On Jul.25.2007 By John Feldhouse

All Horns Blazing
On Jul.22.2007 By Armin

Beckham Colonizes the Galaxy
On Jul.18.2007 By Joe Marianek

the design encyclopedia

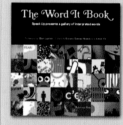
Underconsideration homepage, the umbrella company for all Vit and Gomez-Palacio's web businesses.

ARMIN VIT & BRYONY GOMEZ-PALACIO
UNDERCONSIDERATION LLC

*A*rmin Vit and Bryony Gomez-Palacio are graphic designers who cofounded UnderConsideration LLC in Brooklyn, New York, which publishes the websites Speak Up, The Design Encyclopedia, Brand New, and Quipsologies, and books on design. This husband and wife team lecture, conduct workshops, and teach at the School of Visual Arts in New York.

What was your original impetus for starting UnderConsideration? And did you foresee the various offshoots it would have?

AV: In the very beginning, Speak Up was my personal reaction against the somewhat distorted, one-sided appreciation of what design was during the heady days of the dot-com era, where beveled buttons, exploding 3-D polygon graphics, and Flash animations were being touted and celebrated online as "design." At that time, design portals were being created by Web designers with no appreciation or acknowledgment of traditional (non-Web) design. As someone who was trained in the traditional way but "schooled" in the Web in my first two years as a professional, I realized I could create a collaborative space online where traditional graphic design could be appreciated and showcased in this new medium. From there, in its lack of activity in that first iteration and the early advent of blogging, Speak Up took shape as a space for discussion. Five years ago, I would have never guessed I would be running three blogs and one wiki. Had I foreseen it and realized the amount of work it was going to take to fuel the sites, I would have probably kept my mouth shut.

What skills did the two of you have as designers, technologists, writers and so on, to make you feel that you could do this?

AV: The only skill I had going into it was being an angry designer who had spent his first twenty years being quiet and all of a sudden had this urge to yell. I couldn't code really well back then either, so it was all patched-up work. The beauty about Movable Type when it came out was that it leveled the field. Anyone who could follow a set of instructions could launch a blog, so in my increasing appetite for learning the workings of the Web, I found a great way of releasing some of the geekiness that was boiling inside me. Eventually, once Speak Up was running and it relied on writing, I realized I had never written anything longer than an email. And English was my second language. So as a writer, I had no skill that would indicate that I could do this. I have developed it on the go, and there is no better way to acquire a skill than just doing it. Nowadays, I suffer from overconfidence in the way I write, design, and code, so I use that to set harder goals and continue challenging myself.

BGP: I am very task oriented and love to plan and execute items as I check them off my lists. When we realized Speak Up was growing and UnderConsideration was starting to play a major role in our endeavors, it became increasingly important to manage all aspects of what we were doing. I also participate on the public side as an author across all sites and Word It "master."

The blog business does not bring in profit, at least it hasn't. So how do you fund your efforts? And what are your plans for future financial gain?

Homepage of the daily blog Speak Up (underconsideration.com/speakup), which was the first such design community website launched. Design and programming: Vit.

Homepage for The *Design Encyclopedia* a Wikipedia-inspired structure that invites readers to contribute their knowledge on myriad design themes. Design and programming by Vit. Extra programming: Su, House of Pretty.

(Top) A winning poster design by Tristan Benedict-Hall, for a Speak Up design contest. Participants were asked to select a comment from anywhere on Speak Up and illustrate it. (Above) *The Word It Book*, published in April 2007, includes over 1,500 "Word Its" Book design: Gomez-Palacio.

AV: A few years ago, we started carrying banner ads on Speak Up, and we had a small amount of success in getting a few advertisers on our own, which brought in some income, some of which we funneled into our *Stop Being Sheep* publications. We were able to kick-start projects like our poster and T-shirt contests, where we had to put money up front and hope that we could at least break even. When we launched *The Design Encyclopedia*, we asked Veer (our long-time friends and supporters) if they were interested in funding the first year, which allowed us to hire a programmer and build the wiki.

BGP: Most recently, with our four sites in full swing, we hired a marketing firm to help us establish an advertising plan and lure advertisers to place banners on our network of sites, which is a great thing to be able to offer. So far, the results have been promising.

Let's talk passion. Would you say that the various UnderConsideration components equal a passion for the two of you? In other words, is this more about love than money?
AV: They equal a passion in the sense that we've found something that we can do together that is out of the norm for a couple. We get excited about UnderConsideration. We lose sleep over it together. And we've built it together. I wouldn't call it love over money (as I would love more money from this). I would call it, for me, curiosity over money. To see how far we can push these ventures and see what else spins off. I love that everything we've done so far has been informed by what has come before it.

BGP: It is a bit of a building blocks game for us, pushing the height of the stacks until they can't hold another piece and we have to start a new tower. We find pleasure in the self-imposed challenges and in exploring new areas and setting new boundaries.

{ ANGELA VOULANGAS & DOUGLAS CLOUSE

TYPEHIGH GREETING CARDS

*A*ngela Voulangas received her BA from Yale and is a designer and writer in Brooklyn, New York. Doug Clouse is a designer and teacher who curated an exhibition on the designer Alvin Lustig at the Bard Graduate Center, where he completed a master's degree in design history. typeHigh is rooted in their love of letterpress printing. While waiting for typeHigh to go global, the duo is collaborating on a book about nineteenth-century design to be published by Princeton Architectural Press.

What inspired both of you to create letterpress greeting cards?
DC: Inspiration came from nineteenth-century type samples in antique specimen books. We liked them so much, we thought others would as well.

AV: I really had the urge to do something "crafty" and handmade. I also liked the almost surreal quality the specimens had. We thought it was a different approach for letterpress cards rather than the many birds and babies motifs one sees out there.

Did you enter this entrepreneurial activity with the idea of creating a business and making a profit?
DC: Profit was a goal—especially in the flush of first inspiration, when one imagines unlimited success. At the least we want to cover expenses.

What did you have to learn about the stationery business that you did not already know?
AV: There are a lot of people doing letterpress. There are things to be aware of, such as packaging groups of cards and realizing that some cards might be boring to us, but they end up selling. Then the considerations involved in fleshing out our business persona, like stationery and mailing labels, for example. These are things that I didn't really think about ahead of time.

To what extent is this part of your daily routine? In other words, how much of your work is client driven versus entrepreneurial?
DC: Selling on Etsy.com requires daily checks of the site. Sales are influencing what new designs we are planning.

What determines the style of your cards?
DC: A sense of history, fascination with the nineteenth-century, and humor.
AV: And I really like oddity!

How related is this work to your client-driven work?
AV: This is totally unrelated to what I do. It is an outlet.

How successful are your cards? And where do they sell?
AV: They're in a couple of small shops here in New York City and one in Los Angeles. Right now we're on Etsy.com. It's a lot of hard work to keep pushing your wares.

Do you see a point where you'll have more and different "lines" to the business?
AV: I'd love to branch out but keep the art direction consistently quirky, historically based, ornamental. I'd like to be a one-stop shop for nineteenth-century-inspired ornamental whatnots.

Selected Letterpress creations from typeHigh: stationery, product and packaging, and cards. Design: Angela Voulangas and Douglas Clouse.

DOUG CLOUSE | ANGELA VOULANGAS
TYPEHIGHPRESS@GMAIL.COM

LUCKY
magnet

HEY

AGE
EXPE
ALW

DROP
ctie for
STIN

DELICATE
LOVE'S BOUQUET

{ MATTHEW WALDMAN

NOOKA WATCHES

Matthew Waldman is the president of Berrymatch in New York City, an interdisciplinary design studio that crafts corporate identities and design systems for a wide array of clients. He is also a fine artist exhibiting his work at galleries around the world. He is the designer, founder, and creator of Nooka watches.

Why did you found Nooka?

I founded Nooka Inc. as a stand-alone entity to better focus on developing the brand and market, whereas originally the Nooka watch was just a project I produced with my design studio, Berrymatch. When I started, I didn't understand that design consulting and producing actual product are treated so differently in terms of accounting, so setting up Nooka on its own was a necessity as well.

And did you fund the start-up on your own?

Yes. I had sold my apartment in Chelsea in 2003, but didn't jump back into the market. At the time, Seiko held the license to my watch designs, but the company went through a reorganization where they shed most of their subbrands. I was working as the creative director at Reuters at the time and was frustrated with both the job and the turn of events with Seiko. After complaining about the Seiko issue to everyone I knew, a friend suggested that I do the watches on my own, which was a breakthrough moment, as I had never even entertained such a thought. After a bit of research on how much

it would cost to do two models in limited 1,000-piece editions, I came up with a number that was lower than I imagined. I then decided that this would be a fun way to invest some of my money. I politely cancelled my contract with Seiko and set out to produce my first edition.

What does Nooka mean?

Nooka is a contraction of "New Yorker" with a Brooklyn accent. But moreover, I wanted to create a name that is borderless, could be Scandinavian, could be Japanese, and always conveys "new." I call it *Nooismo*.

What is the investment in time, energy, and money to produce the NHB and NVW watches?

It takes about four months from sketches to a working prototype. Then another two months to produce an order. There are molding charges for the case and components as well as charges to make a custom circuit board and resulting LCD that you have to amortize against the quantity of the life of the product. In terms of energy, you need a lot of it, as dealing with factories continents away

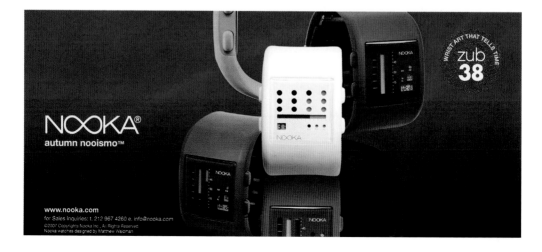

can be both time-consuming (midnight conference calls and trips) and emotionally draining. In terms of dollars, I invested $80,000 to develop the first line, resulting in 2,000 pieces, including the first website and support materials.

Where did the idea come from?

It came from a flashback I had while waiting for a client in a hotel lobby in London in 1997. I was creative director of an interactive design studio and obsessed with the new field of information architecture and intuitive design. While staring at the wall clock, I remembered learning how to tell time in first grade. We even had time-related math homework on those blue mimeographed sheets. How intuitive is a clock if someone has to teach it in school? Surely there are other ways to display time that are more intuitive? I then started sketching on a napkin and thus the Nooka was born.

I love the slogan, "Wrist art that tells time." How are they doing in the marketplace?

Overall, I'd say we're doing very well, though the experience is different in each market. For example, we are not doing as well as I'd like here in New York City, but selling very well in Los Angeles. We do great in Japan, but we're having a slow time in Europe. We are a young start-up and still learning.

Your press images emphasize sexuality and sensuality. Does this accurately represent your targeted audience?

Yes and no. Our target audience is so broad that it would be difficult to create an image that appeals to everyone. So while it may not accurately represent our audience, it accurately represents our brand and approach.

Have you set a time for success? In other words, have you given yourself a window in which to make this work or not?

Yes, three more years. To me, this is a five-year project, and we are in year two.

"Wrist Art that tells time."
Two different styles from the
Nooka collection.

(Left) Advertisement for the
Nooka watches line.

CHAPTER 4

ONLINE
RESOURCES

DESIGN BLOGS

AIGA VOICE

VOICE.AIGA.ORG

*Newsletter for the American Institute of
Graphic Design.*

Core77

CORE77.COM

The industrial design supersite.

Design Observer

DESIGNOBSERVER.COM

*Features writings about design and culture
from some of the most well-known designers.*

DesignSponge

DESIGNSPONGE.COM

*Reviews, articles, features, rants, and raves on
all things design related.*

Coolhunting

COOLHUNTING.COM

*A daily update on ideas and products in
the intersection of art, design, culture, and
technology.*

Mocoloco

MOCOLOCO.COM

*Site for modern and contemporary
design news.*

SpeakUp

UNDERCONSIDERATION.COM/SPEAKUP

*An open forum to discuss matters related to
graphic design.*

Supernaturale

SUPERNATURALE.COM

*An independent site dedicated to the do-it-
yourself culture.*

SVA MFA Design Podcast Series

DESIGN.SCHOOLOFVISUALARTS.EDU/WEBLOG

*Includes podcasts on visiting guest lectures,
Steven Heller lectures on design history, a
showcase of MFA Designer as Author students
discussing their thesis projects, and more.*

Unbeige

MEDIABISTRO.COM/UNBEIGE

Media bistro's design blog.

REFERENCE

Design Addict
DESIGNADDICT.COM
History of twentieth century design, virtual exhibitions, designer, and manufacturer index, links, etc.

Digital Thread
DIGITALTHREAD.COM
A hub of graphic design links for the global Web design community. Includes design firms, portfolios, studios, books, and resources.

Netdiver
NETDIVER.NET
A digital culture magazine devoted to tutoring, empowering, and stimulating creativity as well as excellence in design projects by the international community.

Thomas Net
THOMASNET.COM
Online compendium of products and services, searchable and browsable by categories.

Small Parts
SMALLPARTS.COM
Online catalog for hardware for researchers and developers. Cutting tools, fasteners, adhesives, storage products, etc.

Vitamin
THINKVITAMIN.COM
A resource for Web designers, developers, and entrepreneurs. Includes interviews, articles, and reviews on Internet start-ups, design entrepreneurs, and trends. The advisory board includes many design entrepreneurs, such as the individuals behind Flickr and Threadless.

Colour Lovers
COLOURLOVERS.COM
Resource that monitors trends in color for designers. Can download color palettes that other users share with the community.

CUSTOMIZED ONLINE PRODUCTS
The following sites all offer similar services:

CAFEPRESS.COM
set up your own store of customized products.

ZAZZLE.COM
a printing company using images you upload directly.

MOO.COM
a printing company using images you upload directly.

SPREADSHIRT.COM
design, buy, and sell customized shirts.

MATERIALS

Canal Plastics
CANALPLASTICSCENTER.COM
Custom fabrication, cutting, and engraving services.

Material Connexion
MATERIALCONNEXION.COM
Extensive knowledge base for information about new and innovative materials.

T & T Plastic Land
TTPLASTICLAND.COM
Professional acrylic fabrication, and precision cuts, and shapes.

The Complete Sculptor

SCULPT.COM

Source for tools, supplies, and services relating to sculpture.

....

PACKAGING

The Container Store

CONTAINERSTORE.COM

Offers every type of container for purchase in small quantities.

SDS bottles

SKS-BOTTLE.COM

Great resource for all types of bottles and vials in bulk.

USBOX.COM

Resource for all types and sizes of boxes.

....

SELF-PUBLISHING

LULU.COM

Offers innovative, scalable publishing solutions. Upload your PDF to publish.

QOOP.COM

QOOP turns digital content into products. They also provide real-time printing of blogs and other online content.

BLURB.COM

Using the drag-and-drop-type BookSmart software that you can download from the Blurb website for free, you can design and publish your own Blurb book.

MYPUBLISHER.COM

Similar to Blurb, using their own software to help you design and publish your book.

BOOKBINDING

There is a center for book arts in just about every city. Great way to learn how to put together your own book.

San Francisco Center for the book

SFCB.ORG

Center for Book Arts in New York

CENTERFORBOOKARTS.ORG

Online Bookbinding Tutorials:

PHILOBIBLON.COM/TUTORIALS.SHTML

....

INTERIOR AND FURNITURE DESIGN

e-interiors

E-INTERIORS.NET

Geared towards architects and interior designers, this website catalogues information on top Italian and European furniture designers. In addition, they offer free downloads of 2D and 3D CAD files for most products.

House of Design

HOUSE-OF-DESIGN.NL

A catalogue of (mainly Dutch) jewelry, furniture, lighting, and accessories designers.

Kit3Dmodels

KIT3DMODELS.COM

3D furniture models in Max and DXF format.

ONLINE PRINTING COMPANIES

Options for low-cost, digital printing with a quick turnaround:

OVERNIGHTPRINTS.COM

VISTAPRINT.COM

4OVER4PRINT.COM

PRINTPLACE.COM

....

RETAIL

Elsewares

ELSEWARES.COM

Place to buy and sell independent design wares.

Shop Orange Button

SHOPORANGEBUTTON.COM

An online shop from Nest, supporting women artists and artisans in the developing world by helping them create sustainable entrepreneurial businesses.

Design Sponge Shop

DESIGNSPONGESHOP.COM

Showcase of affordable, limited-edition designs by independent artists.

Etsy

ETSY.COM

Place to sell and buy all things handmade.

Trunkt

TRUNKT.ORG

Buyer's guide to independent art and design.

Charles and Marie

CHARLESANDMARIE.COM

Distributors of unique, well-designed products.

TinyShowcase

TINYSHOWCASE.COM

They sell one limited-run, small print per week. Formed to connect art lovers who have small budgets with artists who want to get their work "out there."

RareDevice

RAREDEVICE.NET

This storefront is a place to promote designers, artists, and artisans plus help them grow by taking on new projects and collaborations.

Sampler

HOMEOFTHESAMPLER.COM

This is a marketing and promotional tool for independent designers. Designers send in samples of their products and promotional materials and subscribers receive a monthly box of contributions from those designers. Frequent submissions include stationery, craft kits, accessories, soap, buttons, etc.

....

LEGAL

US Patent and Trademark Office.

Includes an electronic search system.

USPTO.GOV

Copyrighting tools and information.

COPYRIGHT.GOV

DESIGNER INDEX

Eve Kitten
Nancy Bacich
www.evekitten.com

FUSEPROJECT
Yves Behar
www.fuseproject.com

Gary Panter
www.garypanter.com

HDR Visual Communication
Hans Dieter Reichert
www.hdr-online.com
www.baselinemagazine.com

James Victore Inc
www.jamesvictore.com
www.victorenyc.com

Jesse Willmon
www.jessewillmon.com
www.com-mix.org

Jessica Jackson
jessicalena78@yahoo.com

Jet Mous
www.jetmous.nl

Jones Knowles Ritchie
Andy Knowles
www.jkr.uk

Julian Montague
www.montagueprojects.com

Kidrobot
Paul Budnitz
www.kidrobot.com

Kubaba Books
John Bigelow Taylor
Diane Dubler
www.kubaba.com

Landers/Miller Design
Rick Landers
www.landersmiller.com

Little Fury
Tina Chang
Esther Mun
www.littlefury.com

Little School of Moving Pictures
Barbara Ensor
www.littleschoolofmovingpictures.com

Louise Fili Ltd.
Louise Fili
www.louisefili.com

M + Co
Maira Kalman
www.mairakalman.com

Marshall Arisman
www.marshallarisman.com

Maryland Institute College of Art
Graphic Design MFA Program
Ellen Lupton
www.mica.edu

McSweeney's
Dave Eggers
store.mcsweeneys.net

Metzner Productions
Jeffrey Metzner
www.stick-stuff.com

Mike Mills Diversified
Mike Mills
www.humans.jp
www.mikemillsweb.com

The Miraculous San Honesto Inc.
Luisa Gloria Mota Velasco
www.sanhonesto.com

Modern Dog Design Co.
Robynne Raye
www.moderndog.com

Nooka Inc.
Matthew Waldman
www.nooka.com

ACKNOWLEDGMENTS

We are indebted to our Rockport Publishers editor Emily Potts for her attention to detail and overall encouragement. Thanks so very much to Rick Landers, whose lively format and sprightly design imposes unity on this book's disparate material and brings the entire project to life.

We could not have accomplished our goals if not for Lara McCormick, our trusted associate and amanuensis and Sophie Lee, who assisted in the early stage of the project, and Theresa Rollison, who helped in the later stage.

We also offer a tip of the hat to Regina Grenier at Rockport Publishers for making sure all the pieces are in place.

Our very special acknowledgment goes to David Rhodes, President of the School of Visual Arts, for his tangible aid to this project, but mostly for his constant encouragement for our Designer as Entrepreneur MFA program in general, and the ideas and products he's supported that have emerged from our faculty and students.

We are also grateful to our associates at the School of Visual Arts MFA Designer as Author program, Esther Ro-Schofield and Matthew Shapoff, for their loyal support and continual assistance.

Much appreciated were the generous referrals of design entrepreneurs contributed by our friends Paola Antonelli, Randy J. Hunt, Elana Dweck, Marc Rabinowitz, and Dror Benshetrit.

Finally, thanks to all the designer/entrepreneurs who generously contributed to this project. Your work has been an inspiration to us all.

– SH & LT.